ARMOR *Series*

VOLUME 3

GOD'S
ARMOR
BEARER

*Running with
Your Pastor's Vision*

ARMOR BEARER Series

VOLUME 3

GOD'S ARMOR BEARER

*Running with
Your Pastor's Vision*

TERRY NANCE

Destiny Image Publishers, Inc.

P.O. Box 310
Shippensburg, PA 17257-0310

"For where your treasure is, there will your heart be also."

ISBN 0-7684-2299-X

For Worldwide Distribution
Printed in the U.S.A.

2 3 4 5 6 7 8 9/ 09 08 07 06

This book and all other Destiny Image, Revival Press, MercyPlace,
Fresh Bread, Destiny Image Fiction, and Treasure House books are available
at Christian bookstores and distributors worldwide.

For a U.S. bookstore nearest you, call
1-800-722-6774.

For more information on foreign distributors, call
717-532-3040.

Or reach us on the Internet:
www.destinyimage.com

Dedication

I dedicate this book to my lovely wife. Kim, you have stood faithfully with me for 26 years in seeing the call of God fulfilled in my life. I could never have made it without you. You have been a strength and encouragement to me in all I have ever attempted to do. You are a great woman of God and I love you very much. *Love will keep us together.*

Table of Contents

Introduction

In 1983 I was faithfully working in a local church as an associate minister and mission director. My wife and I were excited to see the first mission students being released and sent out from our church. It gave me a great feeling of satisfaction that the mission school we had raised up was producing what we had envisioned it to do.

Several months after our first group of students had been sent out, I was relaxing at home one night with my wife. We had been visiting about the future and what we felt the Lord was leading us to do. As I sat there I suddenly began to sense an urgency to go and pray. I felt the Lord had something to say to me and I knew I must get alone.

I went into my living room, sat in a chair and simply asked the Lord, "What are you saying to me?" I heard in my heart the Lord say, "Go read the story of David and Saul." I quickly turned in my Bible to First Samuel and read through the first 16 chapters. As I read I came to First Samuel 16:21, "So David came to Saul and stood before him. And he loved him greatly and he became his armorbearer."

As soon as I read that scripture I heard the Lord say to me in my heart, "I have called you to be an armorbearer to your pastor." At first I did not understand what that meant, but as I reread about Jonathan and his armorbearer I began to see what God was saying to me.

I knew the Lord was giving me an assignment that night to stand with my leader and be a support to him. When I began to realize this I slipped out of my chair and laid on the floor. I cried out to the Lord and said, "Now Lord wait just a minute, what about my vision for the world that you gave me before I ever met my pastor?" The Lord said that night for me to lay down my vision and take up the Vision of the House. He said He would take care of the vision I had for the world. He reminded me of His example in coming to the earth. He laid down His desires and took up the Father's, and God highly exalted Him. What you make happen for someone else God will make happen for you.

What is the Vision of the House? It is the vision the Lord has placed in the heart of your pastor. When God gives an assignment to build a church He will always place a calling in the heart of a man or woman of God to birth that local church. With the calling comes a word that will be the mission statement for that local body. That is the Vision of the House. Once it is communicated it is time for those who are a part of that local church to get plugged in and begin to use their gifts and talents.

When you place your vision under the Vision of the House you will begin to see the Holy Spirit bring to pass what God has put inside your heart. This commitment will be one of the major keys God will use to unlock your future. My wife and I are a testimony of this revelation. We have seen God fulfill our hearts' desire when we made a decision to run with the vision of our local church.

I believe the local church is God's idea and not man's. God has set the local church in these last days to be one of the major players in this last day harvest. I do believe this is the hour of the local church.

My prayer is that, as you read this book, you will be challenged and stirred to get plugged into your church like you never have before. I pray God stirs your heart to stand with your pastor and to make a new commitment to do the will of God in your life. As you join heart and soul with the other members in your church you will begin to witness God's power in an unprecedented way. You are called to be not just a member, but a minister.

May God bless you and take you to a new level in your spiritual walk. May you become a participator and not just a spectator.

Chapter 1

IT'S TIME TO...
GET PLUGGED INTO THE POWER SOURCE

Have you ever considered how far faithfulness could take you?

We show up at our jobs each day, not always seeing what our faithfulness is creating for our futures. We go to church each week, sometimes not realizing the character, power, and stability that our faithful actions are producing—not only in our lives, but also in lives throughout the world.

Have you ever considered that faithfulness to your local church touches lives throughout the world? It does; and as you read this book, you'll understand why. In fact, your total understanding of faithfulness will probably change.

Faithfulness is a spiritual law that when activated, produces tangible evidence in our lives. With every person who has accomplished something great in the world or in the Church, you'll find that person was faithful to something. Their mark of greatness began with and continued through a lifestyle of faithfulness.

William Bradford, one of the most influential founders of America, left a matchless legacy of Christian ethics and political leadership that began with a seemingly small act of faithful church attendance. His life exemplifies Luke 16:10a (KJV), "He that is faithful in that which is least is faithful also in much."

Bradford, born in Austerfield, England in 1590, was orphaned at a young age. He spent the remainder of his childhood shuffled from one relative to another. At age 12 he began attending the Puritan Church in Babworth. Despite the beatings he received for attending, he walked eight miles each Sunday to go to church. It was this commitment to faithfulness that provided the momentum of Bradford's life.

By the age of 17, Bradford was a fully committed member of the church. Soon persecution arose against the group for their radical separatist views. As the rest of the congregation successfully fled from England, Bradford was caught and imprisoned for his beliefs.

After a short prison stay, Bradford was successful in his flight from England, and joined the rest of his church in Holland. Although they could now worship according to their own beliefs and were free from the Church of England's restrictions, Bradford and the congregation spent the next 12 years living in near poverty.

Religious persecution followed these faithful believers and they found that all of Europe would be intolerant of their beliefs. There was no safe haven, and it appeared there was only one way out. Through God-given passion, the congregation made the decision to leave everything they knew, and to relocate in the Americas.

Bradford, now 30 years old with a wife and young son, shouldered much of the administrative and organizational work involved in the Mayflower voyage. He sacrificed so much—forced to leave his son in Europe and the death of his wife while on the journey to America—to ensure the freedom of religious worship for his people.

Arriving in New England (not northern Virginia, as was their original destination), Bradford assisted in drafting the Mayflower Compact. This document, one of the most important in America's history, was the first civic law of the emerging nation.

In the name of God, Amen. We whose names are underwritten, the loyal subjects of our dread sovereign Lord, King James, by the grace of God, of Great Britain, France, and Ireland King, Defender of the Faith....

Having undertaken, **for the glory of God, and advancement of the Christian faith,** *and honor of our King and Country, a voyage to plant* *the first colony in the northern parts of Virginia, do by these presents solemnly and mutually, in the presence of God, and one of another, covenant and combine our selves together into a civil body politic, for our better ordering and preservation and furtherance of the ends aforesaid; and by virtue hereof to enact, constitute, and frame such just and equal laws, ordinances, acts, constitutions and offices, from time to time, as shall be thought most meet and convenient for the general good of the Colony, unto which we promise all due submission and obedience. In witness whereof we have hereunder subscribed our names at Cape Cod, the eleventh of November, in the year of the reign of our sovereign lord, King James, of England, France, and Ireland, the eighteenth, and of Scotland the fifty-fourth. Anno Domini, 1620 (emphasis added).*

Bradford's was the second name signed under this declaration. One of the original founders of the Plymouth Colony, Bradford governed the colony for nearly 36 years after the death of John Carver, until his own death in 1657. Bradford is sometimes called "the father of American History" because of his work, *The History Of Plymouth Plantation*, detailing the Mayflower voyage.

It is almost an understatement to say that William Bradford's life influenced scores of people. His political and administrative skills were the foundation upon which the nation of America was built. His courageous sacrifice in the pursuit of religious freedom is the backbone of freedoms that many nations enjoy today. His perseverance and vision still inspires many to reach their dreams and visions.

These characteristics were developed during his early years, when the only control he had over his life was a steadfast faithfulness to his church.

ᛝᛝᛝᛝᛝᛝᛝ

Some time ago I purchased an expensive dual voltage hair dryer for international travel. My family knows how much I like it and that it is off

1 3

limits to everyone but me. Due to the kind of hair I have, it is necessary that I use a hair dryer every day. This can only be appreciated if you could see me when I first wake up in the morning! This dryer was designed to meet my need and I never leave home without it.

However, no matter how much I paid for it, no matter how well designed or how well-crafted it is, no matter how much I enjoy it, this hair dryer will not work unless it is plugged in. I can talk about how nice it is, but if I don't plug it in, it is nothing but an expensive, useless piece of plastic.

Many Christians today can be compared to this hair dryer. God designs them with gifts, talents, and abilities, but because they are not plugged in, they sit on the shelf never doing what God designed them to do.

THE LOCAL CHURCH IS LIKE AN ELECTRICAL OUTLET

Like electricity, the Holy Spirit is the conduit to the power of God. Just like electricity flows through wires waiting to bring life to appliances, the Holy Spirit is always flowing, waiting to bring life to anyone who will plug in.

The local church is the outlet the Holy Spirit uses to train and equip the saints for the work of the ministry. God places leadership over us to prepare us to fulfill His calling on our lives. However, it doesn't matter how much the Holy Spirit is flowing, or how great and anointed the outlet (church) is—like electricity through wire—*nothing happens until we plug in.*

Not forsaking the assembling of ourselves together, as is the manner of some, but exhorting one another, and so much the more as you see the Day approaching (Hebrews 10:25).

The definition of the word *forsaking* is "to desert or leave." People desert the local church for many reasons:

- They are offended.
- They are rebellious and cannot submit to spiritual authority.

• They have allowed the spirit of the world to be a stronger influence in their lives than the Spirit of God.

• They have been under abusive spiritual authority.

In most cases, these deserters have backslidden and most don't even know it. I accept the fact that there are some legitimate reasons why people have left a particular church. I also realize that there are some leaders who are so controlling that they end up hurting and abusing God's people. In this book I am not dealing with these abusive situations. I am dealing with people who cannot submit their lives into the biblically-ordained care of another. They may not see themselves this way, but they are deserters of the faith because they have no accountability in their lives. They lead a life totally ruled by circumstances, feelings, emotions, and ultimately, satan.

The Word of God gives us many reasons to attend and respect our local churches. The Lord considers the church to be:

• An assembly (Acts 19:39).

• A spiritual house (1 Peter 2:5).

• The house of God (1 Timothy 3:15).

• The pillar of God (1 Timothy 3:15).

• Ground of the Truth (1 Timothy 3:15).

• The habitation of God (Ephesians 2:22).

• The building or holy temple (Ephesians 2:20-21).

• The flock of God (1 Peter 5:2).

• The Bride of Christ (Revelation 21:2).

THE LOCAL CHURCH KEEPS US IN VICTORY

An individual came to see me one day and shared a beautiful testimony of his salvation and deliverance from an extremely sinful lifestyle. It was shortly after his conversion that he shared all the things in which he had been involved. By the leading of the Holy Spirit, I told him that in order for him to remain free of the old sin, he would have to be in church every time the doors opened. Even if he had to walk there, he must make church attendance a priority.

That was over ten years ago. This person did just what the Holy Spirit had me tell him to do and he is still walking faithfully with the Lord, heavily involved in church.

Just recently he reminded me of the conversation and thanked me for that counsel. He said he had made the local church a priority and the determination to *stay in church* kept him victorious. He is now helping others to get free and stay free.

Although I understand that character and gifts are developed in every arena of our life, they are reinforced through involvement in the local church. The local church is vital to our Christian lives because it is:

- Where we learn the foundational truths of the Word of God.

- Where we learn character, stability, and faithfulness.

- Where we discover our gifts and talents.

- Where we discover the unique anointing on our lives.

- Where relationships are established that sharpen us.

- Where we learn to respect and honor the God-called leadership placed in our lives.

- Where we learn how to submit to authority.

- Where our faith in God is matured.

- Where we learn to seek God.

- Where we learn to appreciate our country and honor our flag.

- Where we witness the power of God.

- Where we learn the power of forgiveness.

- Where we raise our children and train them in the things of God.

- The place we call "God's House."

THE LOCAL CHURCH IS THE ARK THAT SAVES THE HOUSEHOLD

By faith Noah, being divinely warned of things not yet seen, moved with godly fear, prepared an ark for the saving of his household... (Hebrews: 11:7).

I was raised in church. We had a golden rule in the Nance house: If the church doors are unlocked, we are inside. I learned early in life that church attendance was not an option.

I remember as a child growing up in church and attending vacation Bible school. I remember pledging allegiance to the American flag, the Christian flag and to the Bible. I remember times as a young boy when my twin brother and I were taken outside and disciplined for misbehaving in church. Today people would scream "child abuse," but it taught me respect for God's house and the Word of God.

It was in church that I was saved. It was in church where I witnessed other people coming to Jesus and began to experience the moving of the Holy Spirit. It was in church where I preached my first sermon.

When I turned 15, I went through a period of rebellion. I did not want to go to church and I didn't think I should have to go. I was running from the call of God on my life. I tested my parents, but found out that I was going to church whether I liked it or not.

My mother was a strong intercessor and she spent a lot of time in her prayer closet for me. One day I told her, "You can lead a horse to water, but you can't make him drink." I thought that was a good statement until she replied, "Well, if the horse stands at the trough long enough he will get thirsty." She was right. I stood there long enough to discover that the waters were sweet and I decided I wanted more.

During my teenage years I stayed out of trouble (away from drugs and alcohol) because every Friday night we were at church. Our pastor had a youth night every Friday to keep us around the church and off the streets. Those times impacted my life and kept me on the right course.

The results of a nationwide survey by Barna Research Group shows that adults who regularly attended church as children, are much more likely to be involved in church-based and personal spiritual activities than those who infrequently attended church when they were young. The study shows that 61 percent of adults who regularly attend church attended as a child, while most of the people who did not attend church as children still do not attend (78 percent).[1]

In church we taste and see that the Lord is good and we desire more. Look at the pockets of revival that are going on right now in our world. Where are they? They are in the local church. Without the local church there is no place for the harvest of souls to be brought in and nurtured.

THE LOCAL CHURCH BRINGS IN THE WORLD HARVEST

The coming of our Lord Jesus Christ is fast approaching. We can clearly see that day is closer now than ever. I believe it is at our door. The Holy Spirit is crying out for His people to get in their places, to get plugged into the outlet He designed as a conduit to His power—the local church. When

---

1. Barna Research Group, Ltd. "Adults Who Attended Church As Children Show Lifelong Effects." *Lasting Impact of Attending Church as a Child.* Copyright November 5, 2001. Date accessed: October 20, 2003 <http://www.barna.org/cgi-bin/PagePressRelease.asp?PressReleaseiD=101&Reference=B>

we are plugged into the outlet, that power will flow through us to touch and change lives.

God is speaking right now to many pastors and church leaders to build bigger buildings to hold the harvest. The harvest will be bigger than any of us can ever dream. The Lord said to me one day, "You cannot stop to build barns during harvest." Every farmer knows it is too late to build then. This is why there are building programs going on all over the country. As church members we need to recognize the importance of a building program in conjunction with our pastor's vision.

Are you one of the members who has been in the way instead of helping to make a way? It is time to get behind our leaders and realize God has raised them up to lead and direct the local church.

Where there is no vision, the people perish...(Proverbs 29:18 KJV).

When people don't get plugged into the local church, they are not hooked up with God's vision. The New King James Version of the above Scripture says that where there is no vision, "*the people cast off restraint.*" These people are actually running wild with no direction.

The only way we can fulfill God's plan for our life is to get plugged into a church with a vision. It restrains us in a godly way, by keeping us focused and running in the right direction. Of course, another definition of *perish* is "to be destroyed or ruined." If we have no direction, we will be ruined.

The focus of this book is *getting plugged into the local church,* so I will refer to this issue only once. To effectively "get plugged into" the local church, each person must first be "plugged into" Christ. The apostle Paul understood this spiritual reality and dedicated the totality of his ministry to getting people "plugged into" (united to) Christ. He understood that if they were plugged into the Lord Jesus then a flow of grace could be created that would enable them to effectively be true members of the Body of Christ. Anything that interrupts that flow will hinder the believer in his ability to relate to himself, his leaders and others in the

Body of Christ. I cannot emphasize this issue enough. Guard carefully your relationship to Christ.

For if we have been united together in the likeness of His death, certainly we also shall be in the likeness of His resurrection (Romans 6:5).

My little children, for whom I labor in birth again until Christ is formed in you (Galatians 4:19).

Now, when we are plugged into the local church, we are plugged into its vision. With no vision we are really out there all alone, with no spiritual support. It is much like being marooned on a desert island. Many things would be taking place around the world—new leaders, wars, natural disasters or technological breakthroughs—but we would be ignorant of all these things because we were isolated. When we are hooked up with a local church, we become aware of how the Spirit of God is moving and what is happening in the spirit realm. New worlds of spiritual reality are opened to us as we begin to relate effectively to the local church. These are things that we cannot discover on our own.

We need to answer the call and realize the harvest is ready. God is pouring out His Spirit in advance of the harvest. We cannot afford to be out of our place and let the harvest rot in the fields.

What we need is commitment. It is God's time to show His glory. We will find it in the local church. It is there that God is raising up people to gather the harvest. He is looking for people who are willing to step up and take responsibility for their place in His plan. And His plan always includes working through a local church.

God help us if we miss this opportunity. I do not want to meet Jesus and have Him ask me why I was someone who resisted what He wanted to do in the church. I want to be able to say, "I ran with the vision of the house that God told me to plug into." When I get to Heaven I want to hear the Lord say, "Well done, good and faithful servant," instead of, "Well?"

Many people don't want to be a part of the church until it changes or the people in it change. We need to pray and ask God to change *us*. A children's minister I know told me a story with an interesting twist. He was praying one day and his prayer was, "Lord bless me and change them." Suddenly, the Lord stopped him and said, "You have it backwards." The minister clearly saw his error and changed his prayer to, "Lord bless them and change *me*." People with this attitude will see the power of God move through them to touch others.

We must be willing to pray that kind of prayer and adopt that kind of attitude. Our prayer should be, "God, bless my church, my pastor and spiritual leaders, and change me." If we will ask God to change us, we will begin to sense the Holy Spirit in a fresh way, and God will bring about a change in our lives.

THE LOCAL CHURCH IS THE INSTRUMENT TO DISPLAY HIS GLORY

To the intent that now the manifold wisdom of God might be made known by the church to the principalities and powers in the heavenly places...(Ephesians 3:10).

God's plan is to allow satan's kingdom to stand back and look in awe at the wisdom of God displayed in and through the Church. You and I are destined to be a part of this Church.

We each have a measure of the wisdom of God in us. When we come together in unity, it becomes a mighty force in the earth that cannot be stopped. When Jesus walked the earth, He was the only Body of Christ at that time. He was not just an apostle, He was *the* Apostle; He was not just a prophet, He was *the* Prophet; He didn't flow in just one of the gifts of healing, He flowed in *all* of the gifts of the Spirit.

For He whom God has sent speaks the words of God, for God does not give the Spirit by measure [to Jesus] (John 3:34).

The Local Church Needs All of Us to Take Our Place

Jesus had the Spirit without measure; He had it all. When Jesus ascended to the Father, He then distributed those gifts to mankind.

Jesus has given each of us an assignment and a place in His Body. Each of us has a part to play. If I do my part and you do your part and the rest of the Body does its part, we will make up an effective and powerful Church in the earth. We will see the full demonstration of the Spirit of God in the earth.

You are in the earth for a purpose. Now is the time to get with God's program. Commit to the assignment God has given your local church. Your contribution to that vision will encourage others as it also enlarges that vision into new dimensions. Be the part God called you to be and watch what will happen. True happiness comes when you are following the will of God for your life.

There is nothing more exciting than being part of a local church and seeing that church reach new levels in the glory of God. That is how the Holy Spirit impacts our cities. As you get plugged in you will learn how to function in harmony with the vision of the local church and realize how to synchronize your life with those around you. Then, you will be amazed at the things you will discover as God begins to give you a vision for your life, and you will also be surprised how that vision complements rather than competes with the local church vision.

We Must Bring Our Vision Under the Vision of the House

Pastor Barry Cook (from Oceanside, California) and I were recently in Mexico City ministering on leadership. While I was teaching, the Holy Spirit revealed a powerful truth to him about the vision of the house. Later that night as we discussed it, the Lord began to unveil more.

An influential Shunammite woman invited Elisha into her house for a meal whenever he passed by. Recognizing he was a man of God, she and her husband made the decision to build an apartment for him on the top of their home.

And she said to her husband, "Look now, I know that this is a holy man of God, who passes by us regularly. Please, let us make a small upper room on the wall; and let us put a bed for him there, and a table and a chair and a lampstand; so it will be, whenever he comes to us, he can turn in there" (2 Kings 4:9-10).

After enjoying the comfort of the room, Elisha sent for the woman so he could express his gratitude for the love and compassion she had shown him. He asked what could be done for her. He wanted the desires of her heart to be fulfilled. When he discovered she had no children, he prophesied to her the birth of a son, satisfying the longing of her heart.

There are several crucial aspects of this story revealing how we, by supporting the vision of the house, can bring our own heart's desire to pass.

1. The Shunammite woman perceived Elisha was a man of God.

If we are going to run with the vision of our local church, we will have to get a revelation of our pastor as a man of God.

Someone once asked Dr. Barry Cook, "What do I need to call you? Do I call you 'Pastor,' 'Doctor,' 'Bishop,' 'Brother Barry,' or just 'Barry'?"

Pastor Cook looked at the young man and said, "Call me by whatever name I speak into your life. If I am your pastor then call me that; if I am doctor then call me that; or if I am just Barry call me that. It is up to you."

I can demand respect in the form of a title, but it will be of no value if I have to demand it. I can speak into someone's life only at the level they will receive me.

If we are going to move into the position God has for us in the last days, we must perceive the men and women of God who have been placed around us and give them the right to speak into our lives. It all starts with recognizing the gifts before us.

2. The Shunammite woman began construction of the prophet's room by removing a wall.

Just like she removed a wall in her home to accommodate the man of God, we must make the decision to allow our pastor to be what he is destined to be in our lives, and the walls will come down. Walls of hurt, rejection, confusion, insecurity, fear, intimidation, or whatever we may have inside, must come down!

When these walls are removed, room is made for a new, fresh anointing to come into our house. If the pastor is free to fulfill his calling, that freedom will open up doors for you to fulfill your calling.

3. The Shunammite woman built Elisha an upper chamber over the top of her house.

Placing the chamber over their home was symbolic of taking the vision of the man of God and placing it over their lives. The vision of the house became their vision when they placed it on top of theirs.

Until we make the same decision to make the vision of our local church a priority, it will never truly be ours. We have to take it and create the proper spiritual place for it in our lives.

4. The Shunammite woman furnished the room with a bed, chair, table and a lamp.

The *bed* represents a place of rest or restoration. When we make the vision of the house our own, we open ourselves for God to begin a restoration process in our lives. That restoration process will create an open heaven of blessings and success in every area of our lives. It will bring us into new and exciting places in our relationship with the Lord.

The *chair* represents us taking our place and position in the Body of Christ. I believe once we adopt the vision of the house as our own, we will find our ideal place of service within the local church as well as new doors of opportunity to serve God in the community around us, and for some it will open doors of ministry to the nations.

However, the chair also symbolizes authority. I see it much like a progressive graduation. Once we have found our place of service and ministry within the church—and submitted to its vision—then the Word of God will continually work through us and character can be built within us. Life lessons—lessons that will come in no other way than by service or ministry through the church—strengthen our integrity and mature our hearts. From the building of that character, integrity, and maturity, spiritual authority is birthed. And with that authority, God can trust us to remedy the situations and circumstances placed before us.

The *table* represents the spiritual food and nourishment that comes only by the Word and the Spirit released in our local church. Each believer should develop the ability to feed himself spiritually. We should, daily, be giving ourselves to prayer, meditation and study of the Scriptures. It is not enough to think that we can survive spiritually by one sermon a week. Having said that, we do need to understand that God has placed into the church pastors/teachers who are especially equipped to enrich our spiritual diet. The teaching of the Word by their ministry will enrich your spiritual diet as they supply you rich, nutritional food from God's Word.

This spiritual feast is prepared by the pastor and his gifts, and by the many guest ministers operating in a variety of the fivefold gifts—the apostle, prophet, pastor, teacher and evangelist. The feast is presented by the variety of ministries made available for our families: The children's ministries, the youth ministries, the single and married ministries, women's and men's ministries, ministry to the elderly, prison and jail ministries, the music ministries. All the ministries within the church create a sumptuous, bountiful table.

Your needs can be met by pulling up to the table. When we allow our pastors and leaders the right to feed our spirits, they will lead us into a deeper walk with the Lord.

The *lamp* purely represents the revelation that will flow into our lives when we give the Holy Spirit His proper priority. These revelations will open the heavens over our lives and will spread into our families.

5. Elisha was blessed by this woman's support and hospitality. To bless her in return, he asked what she desired.

Although the woman never told Elisha the desires of her heart, God knew them. And due to her obedience, she gave birth to a son. Reproduction was the result of the Shunammite woman allowing the vision of God's man to become her vision.

God's will and goal for our lives is reproduction. When we take the vision of the house as our own, we will give birth to many sons and daughters for the Kingdom of God.

Everything I am sharing has been a reality in my own life. God has birthed, by His Spirit, the avenue to establish our lives and ministries in the earth. That avenue is through the local church and its leadership. God is challenging us to a new level of thinking.

Let's take the challenge.

Chapter 2

It's Time to...
Get Out of the Comfort Zone and
Develop the Gift Zone

A Man Just Can't Sit Around
—Chip MacGregor

I suppose most people have dreams, but how many people actually turn their dreams into reality? Larry Walters is among the relatively few who have. His story is true, though you may find it hard to believe.

Larry was a truck driver, but his lifelong dream was to fly. When he graduated from high school, he joined the Air Force in hopes of becoming a pilot. Unfortunately, poor eyesight disqualified him. So when he finally left the service, he had to satisfy himself with watching others fly the fighter jets that crisscrossed the skies over his backyard. As he sat there in his lawn chair, he dreamed about the magic of flying.

Then one day, Larry Walters got an idea. He went down to the local army-navy surplus store and bought a tank of helium and 45 weather balloons. These were not your brightly colored party balloons; these were heavy-duty spheres measuring more than four feet across when fully inflated.

Back in his yard, Larry used straps to attach the balloons to his lawn chair, the kind you might have in your own backyard. He anchored the chair to the bumper of his jeep and inflated the balloons with helium. Then he packed some sandwiches and drinks and loaded a BB gun, figuring he could pop a few of those balloons when it was time to return to earth.

His preparations complete, Larry Walters sat in his chair and cut the anchoring cord. His plan was to lazily float back down to terra firma. But things didn't quite work out that way.

When Larry cut the cord, he didn't float lazily up; he shot up as if fired from a cannon! Nor did he go up a couple hundred feet. He climbed and climbed until he finally leveled off at eleven thousand feet. At that height, he could hardly risk deflating any of the balloons, lest he unbalance the load and really experience flying! So he stayed up there, sailing around for 14 hours, totally at a loss as to how to get down.

Eventually, Larry drifted into the approach corridor for the Los Angeles International Airport (LAX). A Pan Am pilot radioed the tower about passing a guy in a lawn chair at eleven thousand feet with a gun in his lap. (Now that's a conversation I'd have given anything to hear!)

LAX is right next to the ocean and you may know that at nightfall, the winds on the coast begin to change. So, as dusk fell, Larry began drifting out to sea. At that point, the Navy dispatched a helicopter to rescue him. But the rescue team had a hard time getting to him, because the draft from their propeller kept pushing his homemade contraption farther and farther away. Eventually they were able to hover over him and drop a rescue line with which they gradually hauled him back to earth.

As soon as Larry hit the ground he was arrested. As he was being led away in handcuffs, a Television reporter called out, "Mr. Walters, why'd you do it?"

Larry stopped, eyed the man, then replied nonchalantly, "A man just can't sit around."

Although Larry's actions were not carefully thought out, they were brilliantly executed. Thomas Carlyle once said, "The tragedy of life is not so much what men suffer, but rather what they miss." What a great thing Larry would have missed if he had never attempted to fulfill his heart's desire.[1]

---

1. Chip MacGregor, "A Man Just Can't Sit Around," *Stories for the Heart* (Sisters, Oregon: Multnoman Publishers, 1996), 97-98.

The Holy Spirit quickened to me one day that we must step out of the *comfort zone* we are living in and develop our gifts by stepping into the *gift zone*. Then we must be willing to go into the *challenge zone* and run for the *end zone*. Each of us must proceed through this progression if we are going to fulfill the assignment God has given us.

I will be using aspects of a professional football game to illustrate this spiritual principle.

• The *comfort zone* is like sitting in the stands watching the game, but not participating.

• The *gift zone* is like participating in practice sessions.

• The *challenge zone* is actually playing the game.

• The *end zone* is where the points are made—this decides the winner.

This progression can be observed in the life of the apostle Paul.

I have fought the good fight, I have finished the race, I have kept the faith (2 Timothy 4:7).

• Comfort zone—Paul left this zone when he accepted the call of God on his life.

• Gift zone—he fought a good fight.

• Challenge zone—he kept the faith.

• End zone—he finished his course.

THE COMFORT ZONE

The comfort zone is the place in our lives where we have settled in and are no longer growing in our Christian walk and calling. We become complacent—satisfied with where we are with the Lord.

Let's take a look at the characteristics of the comfort zone.

IT IS THE PLACE OF LEAST RESISTANCE

When attending a football game, the only pressure we face is getting the kids ready; getting to the stadium on time; battling the crowds and finding our seats. We know that once we are seated, we are there to relax and enjoy the game. We are not concerned with personally facing the opponent. We can sit and watch the participants deal with the real obstacles.

When we sit in the comfort zone of our Christian lives, the only pressure we face is life itself. We ignore the fact that someday we will stand before Jesus and give an account for the gifts and callings we've received, but haven't used. We are not involved in the local church because we are not interested in added responsibility. And if the pastor talks about commitment, we suddenly feel led to attend another church.

I was asked to preach the funeral of a church member who had passed away. The man, in his 50's, died of a heart attack. When I went in to see his family, I realized I had never met them. While visiting with them, I learned they had attended our church for five years. I was shocked! I was preparing to preach the funeral of a man who had been attending our church for years, yet I had never met him. They would come to church on Sunday mornings and sit in the back of the auditorium and leave immediately when the service was over. They had been offended at their previous church, and to keep from being hurt again, they decided to avoid involvement with church activities and other church members.

These were good people, but they had played right into satan's hands. He kept them from fulfilling the call on their lives because of offense.

I know right now many of you have hurts, wounds or offenses that are keeping you from joining a local church and getting involved. For some of you there might be a valid reason to regroup before you get plugged back into a local church. You probably will need to allow the Great Shepherd to enter the living room of your heart and heal those wounded areas. Remember that you cannot allow bitterness and unforgiveness to cripple your spiritual life. Eventually, you will have to forgive those who have hurt you. You will have to let go of your bitterness. In the end, you are the only one those "evil twins" can damage. Sooner or later, though, you will need to get plugged back into the church so that those wounds can be fully healed.

You must understand that satan wants to keep you crippled and hurting. You are no threat to satan's kingdom with hurt feelings that separate you from the Body of Christ. You are not adequately feeding from a spiritual table that is being prepared for you. Those hurts and offenses are keeping you isolated and holding you hostage from the blessings that are rightfully yours. The Holy Spirit is telling you right now to accurately discern the condition of your life and get involved in your local church again.

If you just sit in the stands, you will never experience the taste of true victory. Total victory is reserved for those who play the game. Ask God to help you and then go talk to those who have offended you and get it corrected. Jesus said to go to the person and make peace with them (see Mt. 5:24). This is the only way to get back in the game.

Satan knows that when we sit on the pew, our gifts and talents are not used and this promotes his kingdom by allowing him to work unhindered. However, when we use our God-given gifts and talents in the work of the Lord, we are destroying satan's kingdom. We cannot let the devil win.

Offense is one of the major obstacles satan sets in our path to prevent us from going forward. He will attempt to get our eyes on people and off of God. He will try to get us involved with disgruntled people so he can change our attitudes and steal our victory. But in the name of Jesus, we must take our stand and refuse to let satan win.

Be strong in the Lord, face the challenges and get in the game. We must determine to win the race God has set before us.

It Is the Place Where You Think Your Opinion Rules

I went to a football game one evening and ended up watching the fans more than the game. My team was not playing well and they were losing heavily.

It was fascinating listening to spectators telling the players how to play the game. One man screamed, "You guys are bums!" He screamed so much that several of the players became agitated at his comments. I looked over at him and wondered what would happen if one of the players, who was twice his size, grabbed him and pulled him over the rail, put a uniform on him and put him in the game. I wondered how well he would do.

It amazes me that church people—who do nothing but sit in their pews—think they have a right to tell the pastor and leadership how to run the church. They think their opinions are the whole truth and that those opinions are the only ones that count. They consider themselves experts, just like the screaming spectators in the stands.

In a ballgame the "experts" are always in the stands. In the church we find the "experts" in the pews. They can always tell you what needs to be done, but they are never doing it.

If you are a church spectator instead of a participant, you do not have the right to give advice or criticize the pastor or leadership. If you are not a tither and are not involved in some form of service in the church, you need to keep your mouth shut. If you are a bystander and not willing to involve yourself in the work of God then your opinions will not have value to the pastor or to God. You need to examine your attitude and judge your heart and ask God to forgive you for what you have been saying and for your superior attitude; then get up and decide to make a difference in your church and start helping others.

It Is the Place Where Most People Live and Die

There are over 300 people mentioned in the Bible. However, I heard John Maxwell teach that only about 20 percent of them fulfilled their assignment and calling.

Matthew 20:16b says, "Many are called, but few chosen." That means everyone is called, but individually we decide whether or not we will become the chosen. It is your choice whether or not you step into your calling. You cannot stand before God and blame anyone else for not fulfilling the call on your life.

In a football game there are always more people in the stands than on the playing field. It is easy to sit and watch a game and never have an understanding of the price the athletes pay to play. The question God is asking each of us now is, are we going to sit and let our lives slip by, or are we going to get out of the comfort zone and make our lives count?

And Terah took his son Abram and his grandson Lot, the son of Haran, and his daughter-in-law Sarai, his son Abram's wife, and they went out with them from Ur of the Chaldeans to go to the land of Canaan; and they came to Haran and dwelt there. So the days of Terah were two hundred and five years, and Terah died in Haran (Genesis 11:31-32).

From this passage it appears that Abraham was not the first man God called to be the "father of our faith." Terah was headed to Canaan, where God later led Abraham. For some reason, Terah just stopped in Haran. He stopped playing the game. He left the realm of competitor and entered the realm of spectator. He died in Haran, his destiny unfulfilled. His name is only listed twice outside of Genesis 11, both in genealogical listings. Abraham's name is found 216 times throughout the Bible.

In the very next verse, Genesis 12:1, the Lord tells Abram to get out of Haran and go to a place God would show him. In other words, it was time to be more than a bystander. When we get off the bleachers and onto the field, God will show us how to play. Abraham did just that and he became the "father of our faith."

The purpose of this book is to stir you up to begin doing something for the Kingdom of God and get plugged into your local church. There is a vision on the inside of you and an assignment God has predestined you to fulfill. Now is the time to start. We must go to our leaders and ask them what we can do to help. The leaders are given to the Body of Christ to equip and assist you in the vision of the house. Your relationships with them will allow their gifts to powerfully influence your life. They will help open your eyes and heart to see God's vision for your church, for your community and for your world. You will find that when you take your place on the field, God will lead you into your gifts and calling.

It Is the Place Where the Opposition Is Not Focused on Us

When we are in the comfort zone the opposition is not concerned about what we are doing. They only focus on the competition—and we are no threat when we are not on the field. We can blissfully applaud and cheer those playing the game and leave without a bump or bruise. However, for someone who is in the game, it's a different story.

When we are playing the game, the opposing team is focused on us. They have studied us, sized us up and know our strong and weak points. They have come prepared to confront us and move us out of the way. They are determined to send us home beaten and defeated.

The Christian who has just joined the game is now suddenly faced with a focused and determined enemy. This enemy lives to defeat us. He will attack the weak points in our lives to get us out of the game and get us out of our churches. This is where the real battle begins. This is why it is easier to sit in the stands and watch the game than get up and join those making a difference on the field. It takes someone who loves Jesus and is willing to fulfill the call of God on his or her life despite the cost.

I recently heard a minister say that if the ministry isn't fun, then God is not in what you are doing. That sounds good, but have we forgotten the cost of the men and women who gave their lives for the cause of Christ? I personally do not think it was fun when Jesus hung on the Cross. I don't think the apostle Paul enjoyed some of the things he went through.

Are they ministers of Christ?—I speak as a fool—I am more: in labors more abundant, in stripes above measure, in prisons more frequently, in deaths often. From the Jews five times I received forty stripes minus one. Three times I was beaten with rods; once I was stoned; three times I was shipwrecked; a night and a day I have been in the deep; in journeys often, in perils of waters, in perils of robbers, in perils of my own countrymen, in perils of the Gentiles, in perils in the city, in perils in the wilderness, in perils in the sea, in perils among false brethren; in weariness and toil, in sleeplessness often, in hunger and thirst, in fastings often, in cold and nakedness—besides the other things, what comes upon me daily: my deep concern for all the churches (2 Corinthians 11:23-28).

This doesn't sound like much fun! And this passage does not mention Paul's beheading, which abruptly ended his ministry. Perhaps more people should read this passage before entering the ministry.

We are here for the cause of Christ and we must be willing to do whatever is required of us to stay faithful to the Lord. There will be times of joy and laughter; but it is time we realize that we have a job to do regardless of what hell throws at us. We are in this game to win.

Then he showed me Joshua the high priest standing before the Angel of the Lord, and satan standing at his right hand to oppose him (Zechariah 3:1).

Zerubbabel and Joshua had an assignment from God to rebuild the walls of Jerusalem. Clearly, an assignment from God, if acted upon, will bring satan's opposition. Just having an assignment does not bring opposition; it is when we attempt to carry out our mission that we meet resistance.

This is why most people sit in the comfort zone. Let's be honest, if we are going to fulfill the assignment of God we will face great opposition. The apostle Paul said in his weakest time God empowered him with His strength.

The Lord spoke to Zerubbabel in Zechariah 4:6b and said, " 'Not by might nor by power, but by My Spirit,' says the Lord of hosts." With the Holy Spirit we always win.

First Timothy 6:12 encourages us to "fight the good fight of faith." What is a good fight? It is a good fight when there is guaranteed victory.

In elementary school I got into a fight with three other boys. I did the smart thing—I ran. As I was running, I saw my older brother on the tennis court next to the school. He weighed about 220 pounds and stood 6'5". I ran to him and grabbed his pant legs, then turned to face the boys chasing me. It was amazing that not one of them came near me. Do you know why? Guaranteed victory! They stopped and stared in disbelief at the size of my brother. They knew their plans to hurt me were doomed to failure and their chances of getting hurt were extremely high.

We have a Father who is for us, so who can be against us? It is time to face the enemy with a renewed faith in our Father. When we get a revelation of the greatness of the Father, we will know we are truly winners.

IT IS A PLACE WHERE MISTAKES ARE NOT COSTLY

We can afford to make mistakes when we are not in the game. We can throw a football around our yard and no one cares whether we catch it or not. However, during a game, catching or missing the ball could make a substantial difference in the final score.

Many Christians don't enter the game precisely because they don't want to face failure. Our society has taught the doctrine of self-esteem for over 20 years. The fruit of this philosophy is a generation that cannot handle the pressure of thinking they are less than king of the hill. This attitude keeps people from even trying. At least on the sidelines they can still "feel" like the king of something.

In our Christian lives, if we choose to sit in the stands and not get involved, we are actually choosing not to submit to spiritual authority. We position ourselves in a place where no one can correct us. We do not have to answer to anyone for what we say or do.

Christians today don't want to be rejected or unpopular. They despise instruction and correction. It is easier to sit in the stands. *Compromise is more comfortable than confrontation.*

However, if something has worth or any real value, it will cost us. In the comfort zone our life really isn't worth much, because we are not paying any price. We are actually living our lives without purpose. We are just sitting in the stands, watching life pass us by.

IT IS THE PLACE WHERE NO VICTORY IS ACHIEVED

In the comfort zone we will never experience the joy of winning. Within every Christian there is a God-given desire to win. We were created by God to feel the joy and excitement of walking and living in victory. That is why when we watch someone win, we desire that same feeling of victory for ourselves. We all have an inward desire to win a race, break a record everyone said couldn't be broken, write a best-selling book or a hit song, or perform an impossible feat that establishes we are the best at something.

These feelings are not from the enemy; they are from God. He wants to stir up creativity inside us so it will bless the people around us. This is God's inborn method of motivating the human race.

But instead of acting on those feelings and desires, too many people sit and think about these things and take no responsibility to bring them to pass. Allowing our lives to be spent watching others succeed and not fulfilling our inborn desire is not God's best for us. When we are in motion, we are on the offensive and we actually receive strength while on the field. When we allow ourselves to be idle, we turn our focus inward, become fearful of failure and just quit trying.

THE GIFT ZONE

The gift zone is a place where you die to your own desires and start serving others.

> *But Jehoshaphat said, "Is there no prophet of the Lord here, that we may inquire of the Lord by him?" So one of the servants of the king of Israel answered and said, "Elisha the son of Shaphat is here, **who poured water on the hands of Elijah**"* (2 Kings 3:11, emphasis added).

Those of us who live in America and Europe do not have a clear understanding of what this Scripture portrays.

I received a revelation of Elisha's role and attitude while I was in Uganda, Africa with missionary Mike Croslow. We were in an area called Pelisa; it took us several hours to get to this remote bush country. It is one of those places that compels you to say, "It may not be the end of the world, but it is certainly visible from here."

As we were preaching, I will never forget all the men, women and children (along with the chickens, pigs and anything else around) who found their way to the service. We had so many people that the service was held outside under a big tree.

Mike and I ministered from early morning until noon. When it came time for lunch I was escorted to the church, which was a simple mud structure with a thatch roof. Attendants brought in lamb, vegetables, millet (grain) and soup.

I looked at Mike and said, "Where are the utensils?" He replied, "Look at your hands because those are your utensils." I laughed and told him I could eat pizza with my hands, but not soup. So, he showed me how the

Ugandans eat. He took a handful of millet, rolled it into a ball, took his thumb and made an indention in the middle of it. Then he put the millet in the soup and ate it with his hands. That was some experience for me, learning to eat soup with my hands.

Just before we ate, a young man walked in with a pitcher of water. He came over to me and poured the water on my hands and washed them. After lunch he returned to perform the same task.

When I arrived back in America, I sat in my office one day and reread this Scripture. Since the culture in Africa is similar to that of the Middle East—they both eat with their hands—the Lord was able to show me something valuable. The Holy Spirit triggered the memory of that young man pouring water over our hands in Uganda, and I realized that Elisha truly was a servant to Elijah.

When you think of the relationship of Elijah and Elisha, the first thing you may think of is *double portion*. I have witnessed people praying for the double portion, seeking God for it and asking ministers to lay hands on them for it; but that is not how it is obtained. Those seeking the double portion need to look for water to pour on the hands of their leader and develop a willingness to serve them. This is where true leadership is born—in servanthood.

Are you willing to pick up the pitcher of water and pour it on your leader's hands?

Elisha literally served Elijah. You can read in First Kings 19:19-21 where Elisha forsook all to follow Elijah. From that day until Elijah's last day on earth, Elisha prepared his meals and took care of him. There is no doubt that Elijah was probably a difficult employer, but Elisha was there for the duration.

When it was time for Elijah to go to Heaven, he asked Elisha what he wanted from him. Elisha looked him in the eye and said, "Please let a double portion of your Spirit be upon me" (2 Kings 2:9b). In other words, "Whatever you've got, I want twice as much."

Elijah knew Elisha meant business. He had remained faithful in the good times and the hard times and that is why he had the right to ask for the double portion.

As I was finishing my first book, *God's Armorbearer*, I asked the Lord to give me a special revelation to conclude the book. The Lord spoke to my heart, *"The Armorbearers of today will be the leaders of tomorrow."* Those who are carrying the water (serving) for their leaders today will be in the forefront of ministry in the years to come.

The problem is that instead of viewing themselves as servants, people would rather serve themselves. People don't see the church as a place where they can serve and meet the needs of others. They see it as a place that should meet their needs; and if it doesn't, they leave.

There are church movements popping up all around that attempt to meet every whim of the member, from the parking spots to the way they preach. This is a disservice to the soon-to-be or new believer. While it sounds kind on the surface, in the long run it can produce selfish, individualistic, cultural Christians.

I wonder how many people would attend a church that Jesus pastored?

IT IS A PLACE WHERE YOUR TRUE GIFTS AND TALENTS ARE DEVELOPED

While a team is on the practice field, they discover their real gifts and talents. Many players initially assume they are going to play a particular position only to discover they are more gifted or needed in another. They have to be willing to allow the coach to decide where they can best benefit the team. Remember, they are there only to serve the interests of the team. They will be unsuccessful if they come to practice with their own agenda.

Too many church members come into a church with their own agenda. They come looking for a place to display their gifts and talents, instead of using those gifts and talents to serve others. And their attitude precludes anyone from telling them where they are needed or if they are correct in their assessment of their own gifts. They are not there to benefit the church but to promote themselves.

A man came into my office one day and shared with me how the Lord was leading him to become a part of our church. He told me that following a season of prayer and fasting, the Holy Spirit revealed to him that it would be from this church he would launch his ministry. He explained to me that he had a gift of teaching and that he would be requiring a place to minister.

I promptly asked him where he was from and with what church he was last affiliated. He wanted to change the subject, but I persisted until he admitted he wasn't connected with any church or organization. I explained to him the process of becoming a member of our church and at that particular time, we would be honored to have him start his ministry in the housekeeping department. Within a few minutes he left my office, and I have never seen him since.

It is on the practice field that our motives are revealed. We may not have the abilities that others have, but we must have the heart to serve. I would choose that heart attitude any day over the gifts and talents of people with the wrong attitude. I cannot think of anyone who came into the church with a servant's attitude who was not eventually elevated into a leadership position or who didn't have other avenues of ministry opened up to them. I would not want to give the impression that all servanthood eventually leads to a place of leadership. That would be too narrow of a perspective. What I am saying is that as you develop the spirit of a servant and as that becomes obvious to those around you, it will eventually lead you into greater spheres of ministry, whether within the context of the church or without. So, rather than focusing on what you should be doing, simply focus in on *how* you should be doing it. Become a faithful servant and that will become a gateway for greater service. This is the way of Jesus.

A Danish proverb says, "*Success in life is not holding a good hand but play-ing a poor hand well.*" The truth is, in life we have to play the hand that is dealt us. We imagine people owe us something, but they do not. We are responsible for our position in life and the decisions we make. *There is no "free lunch."*

Football players make it onto the playing field because they are team players. Their goal is to play in such a way that they are a positive force on the team. Their desire is to contribute their gifts and talents to make a dif-ference in the game.

When we go into the local church to contribute and to be a blessing in that church, then our motives are right and pure—and God will use us. It will not be long before we are promoted into the position in which God has called us.

It Is the Place Where You Learn to Deal With Praise and Criticism

A coach will praise us when we perform well and rebuke us when we are inadequate. He will do whatever it takes to train and motivate his team.

In any local church there are good days and then there are more chal-lenging days. Sometimes the challenging days seem like they will never end. During those times, you must be able to handle the spiritual input from your leaders. Never forget, that God has placed leaders in your life for good, not for evil. They love you and care deeply about your success. If they should see negative attitudes or destructive patterns in your life, it is their spiritual responsibility to help you identify these things and then sup-port you in correcting them. Of course, their input is not always negative. They are also there to confirm you in your journey and equip you for ministry. So, their influence in your life will include both confrontation and confirmation.

Whoever loves instruction loves knowledge, but he who hates correction is stupid (Proverbs 12:1).

I know you may think that God would not say this, but the Bible makes it very clear that a person who cannot receive correction is stupid.

We need to ask ourselves, "How do I react when I am corrected?" If we develop a bad attitude or become offended when unfavorable or uncomfortable situations arise, we need to seek the Lord's help. I have learned this from experience.

The first thing we must do is get alone to pray and let the Holy Spirit speak to us. The Bible says the Lord leads us beside still waters (see Ps. 23:2). So, we must draw near to the still waters, listen to our spirit and let our flesh settle down. Then we need to turn it over to the Lord, let Him tell us where we have erred and then make the necessary correction.

I know that correction and criticism are never easy on the flesh, but we have to make the decision that the vision is more important than remaining offended. It takes no effort to quit and go somewhere else. But it takes a real man or woman of God to stick it out, make the correction and continue on with a good attitude.

Just like there is structure in the family, in leadership, in business and in the church, there is structure in God's world. This is just the opposite of what the world likes to believe. The world hates authority. This is what happened during the Hippie Movement when there was such great reaction to all forms of authority. This movement is called *egalitarianism*, which simply means that we are all equal; there is no authority structure and there shouldn't be any. As the human body teaches us the need for diversity, structure and relationship, so we must understand that for the Body of Christ to function properly she must function along those same lines of relationship, diversity and structure. We are all *not* equal. We are all *unique* in our calling and gifting, and to deny this truth is to destroy the essence of the Body of Christ.

Socialism is fueled by the doctrine of egalitarianism, as is feminism. The recent "child rights" movement is also part of this thinking. Rejection of authority is actually a rejection of God, because He is a God of authority. This kind of social equality cannot work in the world and it won't work in the church. We should celebrate our diversity rather than seeking to force everyone into the same mold.

If a worldly viewpoint remains prominent, the majority of the church will adopt it within 20 years. Egalitarianism is no exception. It has entered the church on many levels. Believers are convinced that they can do an equal, or even superior job next to the church in growing themselves spiritually. This is simply untrue and quite frankly, disobedient to God's Word. This line of thinking totally disregards God's system of government and His design for spiritual covering.

You don't need to be mad at me. God is the one who established rank, leadership and government. He established it for our growth and well-being. It is true that as believers, Christ is our head and we are all equal in spiritual righteousness. However, we are *not all* equal in rank and headship. We are all not placed into the same position. This is the clear message of Paul in First Corinthians 12. How grotesque would it be if we were all a "head" or a "foot"?

For example, a husband and a wife are spiritual equals as a son and daughter in God—but they are *not* equal in rank or headship. The husband is the head of the wife (see 1 Cor. 11:3), and the pattern continues in every phase of our lives. Children submit to their parents (see Eph. 6:1-3); the young submit to the elderly (see 1 Tim. 5:1-2,17); employees submit to employers (see Eph. 6:5-8); citizens submit to civil authorities (see Rom. 13:1-2); believers submit to their local church leadership—and Christ is the head of them all (see 1 Cor. 11:12).

Hebrews 13:17 tells us to obey those who are in responsible church leadership over us, and submit to them according to the Word. They are the ones whom God has appointed to watch for the welfare of our souls, and

He will expect them to give account for us. This verse states that if the leadership can account for us with joy, then it will be profitable for us.

So don't reject the spiritual covering provided by the leadership of the local church. God has designed it to protect you, mature you and nourish you. As the writer of Hebrews says, they are set in place to watch over and guard your souls.

> *Obey your leaders, and submit to their authority. They keep watch over you as men who must give an account. Obey them so that their work will be a joy, not a burden, for that would be of no advantage to you.* (Hebrews 13:17 NIV).

To stay on the right path it is important for us to establish good solid people around us who will be honest and speak the truth in love. I have friends, who know me and are around me all the time, whom I bounce things off of to make sure I am seeing things in a proper manner.

Every so often I will get a letter that is very critical of one of the books I have written. I always give it to my wife and say, "Read this and tell me if it deserves a response." I do not respond to every criticism; if I did, I would waste a lot of time defending myself. When it is personal, it is hard to distinguish between criticism that is valid and criticism that is malicious and unwarranted. This is why I have people around me who can help me stay right in my thinking and my actions.

It would be wise for you to do the same. Don't isolate yourself and think you make up the majority. If that happens, then you will always be right in your own eyes, and all you will hear is your own heart. Don't surround yourself with people who only think like you. There is wise counsel in a multitude of mature and stable believers—and you need to hear all sides in order to make the right choices. You need to surround yourself with godly friends who are spiritually healthy. They are great check-and-balance pointers!

In spite of the challenging days it is vital to always press toward the vision. Always remember the saying, "*Today's mighty oak was yesterday's nut that held its ground."* If we hold our ground, sooner or later we will produce something. If we are faithful, even though we may feel we are lacking in certain gifts and talents, we will produce.

IT IS A PLACE OF GREAT PREPARATIONS

Gifts are never developed overnight.

Just before football season starts and the days are the hottest, two-a-days begin. These are two practices a day, morning and afternoon. This increase in practice sessions may last for several weeks. It will bring out both the best *and* the worst in people.

Double practice actually pushes athletes beyond their endurance. They learn to press on even when both their bodies and minds tell them they are crazy. These practices assist the athlete in developing a mental tough-ness that will allow them to press through barriers when they are pushed past their physical endurance in a game or through injury. The outcome of many games has turned around in the last minutes of play, in favor of the team that is most prepared in these areas.

Unfortunately, this kind of mental toughness is not often evident in many church members today. Too often we go to a church on the basis of what it can offer us, and we will not stay in a church that puts a demand on us to live like the Bible says to live. The words *sacrifice, temperance, restriction, discipline,* and *hardship* are seldom mentioned from the pulpit so that no one is scared away or offended.

> *But I discipline my body and bring it into subjection, lest, when I have preached to others, I myself should become disqualified* (1 Corinthians 9:27).

Paul was talking about the necessity of placing demands upon himself so that he would not give in during times of pressure.

Accomplishing what God is calling us to do in these last days requires a new mental toughness to press through the stress of everyday life. I told my wife recently that we have two options: We can be busy and be happy, or be busy and be full of care; but one thing is for sure, *we are going to be busy!* It is important that I clarify something at this point. We are not called to be "busy" just to be busy, nor are we to be slaves to the old "work mentality" where we derive our self-image out of what we do. Our work must be *directed* work, *purpose-driven* work and work that originates in the will of God.

The other thing we must do is make sure we are all on the same page when it comes to defining "work." We must understand that prayer, meditation and study of the Scriptures is also work. In fact, it is hard work. It is the kind of work that is easy to let go because we don't get as much satisfaction or recognition. But it is the kind of work to which all of us are called. Our "work" must be defined by what God has called us to do. That call can come to us in prayer, and it can also come to us through the voice of our leaders.

When we come to the place where we settle things like this in our minds, then we can face life with the right mental attitude. We must determine in our hearts that we are here to win and we are not going to stop *until* we win. God put us here and He is the only one who can tell us to leave. It is this determination that will cause us to experience the victory that Jesus has already won for us.

If the Holy Spirit has told you to become a part of a particular local church, then that is where you should be. You should feel that your church is the best in the country, that it has the most spiritual and dedicated leadership, where the presence of the Lord is powerfully present, and that the people are the most loving. On the other hand, sometimes God calls us to serve in a church where these things are not evident. Nevertheless, we are called to be there so that by prayer and service we can become a part of a fresh move of God. Start thanking God that you have a church home and begin believing for a new spiritual awakening in it. When you determine these things in your heart, the Holy Spirit will get involved with you and your church.

It Is the Place Where Character, or the Lack of It, Is Revealed

A person's character is proven in times of adversity and challenge.

On the practice field, a football player's real attitudes, strengths and talents are discovered. It is interesting that these strengths and talents are first revealed when they are being tested. True character is exposed during times of opposition.

When we commit ourselves to a local church, our true self will eventually be exposed because we will be faced with the opportunity to get offended, hurt or angry. *The local church is the greatest place to discover just what it means to walk in love.* We become associated with Christians who, many times, have not allowed their minds to be completely renewed, although Jesus lives in their hearts.

I believe one of the major keys to working with people and avoiding offense is by *making allowances for others.* That means allowing them to make mistakes and not holding it against them. The church is a training ground. It is not perfect; we all make mistakes. People will make mistakes, so you might as well accept them regardless. This is the only way you will have peace in life and truly develop God's character. This is why Paul exhorted the Body of Christ *to walk in their calling with all lowliness and gentleness, with longsuffering, bearing with one another in love* (Eph. 4:2).

While you are in the gift zone, you aren't aware that your character is being sharpened. And you just may be surprised at the attitudes that pop out of you. The adversity we encounter in this zone reveals what has been inside of us all along. Then during the game, character is not *developed*—it is merely *displayed.*

Chapter 3

IT'S TIME TO...
STEP INTO THE CHALLENGE ZONE AND RUN TO THE END ZONE

In the long run, men hit only what they aim at.
Therefore, they had better aim at something high.
— *Henry David Thoreau*

From an early age, Larry lived and breathed the sport of golf. As a teenager, he was ranked one of the top 16 young golfers in the nation. Then, at the beginning of his senior year of high school, Larry was in an automobile accident. He suffered severe injuries, but the most devastating was that his left arm had to be amputated just below the elbow.

Larry had never heard of a one-armed golfer, but then again, he didn't know that it couldn't be done! As Larry began to swing a few golf clubs at the rehab center, his mother and a psychologist sought out someone who could design a prosthetic hand for him.

After several months of practice with his new hand, Larry hit a ball one day. When it landed more than 200 yards away, he knew he was "back." He rejoined the high school team, scoring even better than before, and is now in college on a golf scholarship!

"Don't think of your missing limb as something that makes you a lesser person," Larry once told an audience of children who had lost limbs. "Think of it as something that can make you stronger. I would love to be the first pro golfer with a prosthetic hand. But I also know that if I don't succeed, I won't be a failure. We only fail if we don't try."[1]

1. W. B. Freeman Concepts, *God's Little Devotional Book for Leaders* (Tulsa, Oklahoma: Honor Books, 1997), 48-49.

In a football game the challenge zone is the actual game. The number one goal is to win. This is the time we must be better than our opponent. Despite the excitement, a football player will put on what is called a "game face," an expression of someone who is totally focused on the job.

I love the fact that Jesus had a game face. Isaiah 50:7 says that during His torture and crucifixion He *"set His face like a flint."* That means He determined in His heart He would see God's plan through to the end.

Players are not in the game to occupy or amuse themselves; they are there to win. They have studied their opponent and know both his strengths and weaknesses. They know they must perform at their very best to win. There will be no tie in this game. Winner takes all.

> *And Jesus answered and said to them: "Take heed that no one deceives you. For many will come in My name, saying, 'I am the Christ,' and will deceive many.... Then many false prophets will rise up and deceive many"* (Matthew 24:4-5,11).

The disciples had come to Jesus and asked Him about the end of the world. In response, Jesus talked about signs of the end like earthquakes, famines and pestilence. Each of these He mentioned once, but there was one sign he mentioned three times: Deception.

I believe deception is satan's number one weapon against the Church. We live in a day where knowledge is increasing. We see it in the natural, but it is also clear in the spirit. Revelation knowledge is flowing from the Holy Spirit to men and women, giving creative ideas to assist them in reaching the world with the message of Jesus Christ. But with this great revelation comes false teaching and false revelation that quietly slips into the Church and deceives many people.

In a football game, when a team gets within 20 yards of the goal line and is advancing to score a touchdown, the defense will put up what is called "goal line defense." This defense is designed specifically to frustrate the efforts of the opponent when they are very close to scoring. This goal line defense is made up of the strongest, the fastest and the meanest players on the team. Some of these players participate in the game only when the play is near the goal line and a touchdown is imminent. These tough, seasoned players are reserved for the demanding, high-consequence and stressful periods in the game.

I truly believe that satan has deceiving devils he has held in reserve for these last days to keep us from fulfilling our assignments from God. He is now putting in the strongest, the fastest and the meanest devils he has on his team to keep the Church from doing what it has been called to do. Revelation 12:12 (KJV) says that satan knows that he "*has but a short time.*" This is why he will come at us to try to pull us down, get us out of church, away from the goal line, and keep us from fulfilling our call.

The first outward sign of backsliding is always poor church attendance. It happens when the church is no longer a priority in our lives.

You may say, "Well, Brother Terry, my church is dead and that is why I don't go anymore."

My response to you is simple. You need to either pray for your church until Heaven opens over it, or you need to go to a church that is on fire. Either way—get involved. It is too late in the game to be playing around. The Body of Christ must put on their *game faces.*

There are three powerful areas of attack satan has especially prepared to come against the Body of Christ in these last days. These three main areas of attack are causing deception and leading people away from their local church.

In the Letter of Jude we find a list of these spirits. Satan is still using these same three spirits against the Church today, just with different names.

*But these speak evil of whatever they do not know; and whatever they know naturally, like brute beasts, in these things they corrupt themselves. Woe to them! For they have gone in **the way of Cain**, have run* *greedily in **the error of Balaam** for profit, and perished in **the rebellion of Korah*** (Jude 10–11, emphasis added).

This is satan's goal line defense: *The way of Cain, the error of Balaam and the rebellion of Korah.* With these he plans to keep us out of the end zone and from fulfilling our assignment.

Let's take a look at these three spirits and how we can overcome them.

THE WAY OF CAIN

You can read the story of Cain and his brother, Abel, in Genesis 4.

The two brothers had prepared an offering for the Lord, and God had rejected Cain's offering. As far as Cain was concerned, if God rejected his offering, God rejected him.

He then saw Abel's offering accepted by the Lord, and he envied Abel and the blessing that was on Abel's life. Cain had to blame someone but could hardly blame himself; so it must have been Abel's fault that his offering was found unacceptable.

Cain made the decision to eliminate the competition once and for all. So, Cain murdered his brother in a fit of jealousy.

These murderous events were set in motion by the rejection of an offering. Many times in the local church we see someone offering a service or gift that is not welcomed by the leadership. Suddenly, the attitude of that individual changes like Cain's and satan attacks their soul. Their attitude changes because of the same reasoning Cain used, "You reject my gift or talent, you reject me."

People leave their church because they believe the pastor will not let their gifts be used. There are some churches where pastors are insecure and controlling. If this is the case, then you need to simply get into a church where you can trust the leadership and get involved. Don't assume that because you are not asked to be involved in leadership that it is because you are being boycotted or ignored. Perhaps the leadership may feel it is not the right time for that particular ministry or that those talents could best be used elsewhere at the present time. In my own life, I have discovered that if I enter a situation with the attitude that I am here to help in whatever capacity I am needed, it is not long until I am doing exactly what I wanted all along.

The word *rejection* means "to be refused or slighted." When we are rejected it goes against our pride, and if we are not careful, it will lead us into hatred.

> *For this is the message that you heard from the beginning, that we should love one another, not as Cain who was of the wicked one and murdered his brother. And why did he murder him? Because his works were evil and his brother's righteous. Do not marvel, my brethren, if the world hates you....Whoever hates his brother is a murderer, and you know that no murderer has eternal life abiding in him* (1 John 3:11-13,15).

The bottom line is this—to hate is to commit murder in your heart. This is the spirit of Cain. Rejection leads to hurt, offense and then hatred. From there you will find yourselves in the way of Cain.

In First Samuel 16, we can read where Samuel invited Jesse and all his sons to attend a sacrifice. Jesse brought his sons to Samuel and by the instruction of God, Samuel searched through them to find and anoint the next king of Israel. He looked at Eliab, the oldest, and immediately thought that God had picked a fine man to be king—but the Lord stopped him.

> *But the Lord said to Samuel, "Do not look at his appearance or at his physical stature, because I have refused him. For the Lord does not see as man sees; for man looks at the outward appearance, but the Lord looks at the heart"* (1 Samuel 16:7).

One by one the sons of Jesse passed before Samuel, but the Lord refused each of them. After meeting and rejecting all of Jesse's sons, Samuel was confused. He had done as the Lord instructed, but he was unable to anoint any of them.

Samuel finally asked Jesse if he had any more sons and was told of David. David was sent for and when he arrived from the field the Lord told Samuel, "Arise, anoint him; for this is the one!" (1 Sam. 16:12b) David was anointed right there in front of his brothers.

David's attitude through this situation is truly inspiring. Samuel had come to Jesse and asked to meet all of his sons, but Jesse hadn't even thought enough of David to invite him. Here was an unbelievable opportunity to feel rejected and hurt. It would be like not being invited to your family reunion. How would you feel? We would all feel hurt, angry and flat-out mad about it. The normal reaction would be to never associate with those people again.

When David was anointed in front of his brothers, do you think that his brothers gave him any honor? In reading the story of David and Goliath, it is apparent that his brothers despised him (see 1 Sam. 17). I can just imagine what they all said to him after Samuel left, "Go get that oil off your head and clothes and get yourself back to the sheep. Who do you think you are?"

David could have gone back to the field numbed by the negative response he had received from his brothers. He also had the opportunity to be particularly hurt over the rejection of his father. He could have released his anger by kicking a few sheep, or he could have taken an apathetic attitude toward his work in retaliation for his family's disregard, and let the bear and lion kill a few of the sheep.

Instead, David took control of the situation by refusing to allow hurt and rejection to enter his heart. Instead, he put his trust in his heavenly Father. I believe that is why David wrote in Psalm 27:10, "When my father and my mother forsake me, then the Lord will take care of me."

Satan is after our hearts. What is in our hearts will come into the open, so we must guard our hearts at all costs. We cannot allow hurts, rejection and offense to come in and lead us into the way of Cain. There are many people living in a backslidden state today, because they refused to guard their hearts and in so doing opened themselves up to this spirit.

How we face rejection and the negative feelings it brings will determine whether we win or lose in life. In these days we are all going to have to face this attack of the enemy one way or another. In some manner we will experience rejection, whether it concerns our gifts, our children, our families or our own selves. Our response will determine whether we enjoy victory or taste the bitterness of defeat.

We must resolve to immediately turn the situation over to the Lord, choose to forgive, speak that forgiveness out and then go on as if it never happened. It may be necessary to sow a seed of love to break the strongholds of hurt and offense in our lives. Jesus taught us to forgive and do good to them who spitefully use us (see Mt. 5:44). This forgiving stroke breaks the power of the spirit of Cain in our lives and closes the door to hurt and unforgiveness.

While I was still in high school, my parents dealt with a situation within our church involving other people bringing accusations against them. As far as I was concerned, we should have just left those people alone and let the wrath of God take care of them. But my attitude was clearly wrong.

I was shocked one day when my mother fixed a big meal for them. I argued against it, "Why give them anything or be nice to them at all? Don't you remember what they said about you?" But my mother took dinner to them and told them she loved them and then apologized for any misunderstandings they might have had.

Over the next few years God restored their relationship. That same family who once bad-mouthed my parents now calls my mom for prayer. It is amazing that when we do what Jesus said to do, it always works the way He said it would work.

I sense now, as I am writing, that someone needs to do whatever it takes to make it right with either a person or a spiritual leader that has offended you in the past. *If you do not make it right, your hurt will be your ruin.*

You have opened the door to a spirit of Cain and God wants you released from it.

In these last days the love of God must be demonstrated through the Church to the world. We are the Church and we must learn to love people and open up our hearts to all races of people if we are going to fulfill the words of Jesus. The only way this love will be demonstrated is to keep our hearts free from the spirit of Cain.

THE ERROR OF BALAAM

The word *error* means "to go astray." We may start off in the right direction, but subtly we can get off God's chosen path and the spirit of Balaam will lead us instead of the Holy Spirit.

Let's examine Balaam's life and see how this happened. Numbers 22 and 23 tells his story.

Balaam was the son of Beor, king of Edom. Some people believe he was a soothsayer, but the Bible tells us that in the beginning of his ministry, he sought God for the prophecies he gave. His reputation for accurate prophecies sprang from his relationship with God and a right heart.

His fame had reached Balak, king of the Moabites. Because Balak feared Israel, he contacted Balaam to persuade him to use his power to curse Israel and stop them from invading his nation.

Balak sent elders from Moab with material incentives to help convince Balaam to use divination and curse Israel. Pagans knew only of enchantments, magic and witchcraft, therefore, they thought these were the means by which Balaam's words came to pass. Balaam was impressed with what was being offered, so he presented the offer to God. God did not hesitate in answering him.

And God said to Balaam, "You shall not go with them; you shall not curse the people, for they are blessed" (Numbers 22:12).

Balaam had his direction from the Lord, so he immediately obeyed the word of God and sent away the elders of Moab, reward and all. Balaam had done a good job. He had passed the test and felt good about it. But a few days later, the men returned with a promise of riches and honor like Balaam had never seen or heard.

Balaam must have been thinking, *Surely God is about to miss an opportunity to bless me.* This thought had to have entered his heart because he returned to seek the Lord's will—again.

This was the mistake that led him down the path of destruction. God had already given His word. When Balaam went back to the Lord the second time he was not really seeking God's *will,* because he already knew it. Balaam wanted God's *permission.* He knew if he could just return to Moab with the elders, there would be something in it for him. How could God not be in this? It looked too good to pass up. This shows Balaam possessed a love of money, or what Second Peter 2:15 calls the *wages of unrighteousness.*

There are some things to be learned about God in this story. When He says not to do something and you keep pressing Him about it, He will let you do it. His blessing is not in it, His will is not in it, but you *can* pursue it. We must examine our motives to discern if the Spirit of God is leading us or if it is merely our own lust.

A missionary once told me about a Bible school student she had counseled. The student asked if it was all right for her to be sleeping with her boyfriend. The missionary told her, "No!" and then shared some Scriptures with her.

The student responded, "Well, I know what the Bible says, but I have prayed about it and have peace about it in my case." The missionary tried to tell her that since it was in His Word—and the student knew the Word—God was under no obligation to continue to tell her not to do it. Of course, the student went ahead and did what she wanted to do all along.

Today, rather than be guided by the Bible, Christians make moral decisions—including church attendance—based on feeling. The Barna Research Group conducted a survey, which found that only four out of every ten born-again adults relied on the Bible or church teachings as their primary source of moral guidance. When asked the basis on which they formed their moral choices, nearly half of all adults (44 percent) cited it was their desire to do whatever brought them the most pleasing or satisfying results.[1]

We live in a day when people will become whatever you want them to be, as long as you provide for them materially. I heard Dr. Lester Sumrall once say that there are "belly nations." These are countries that will basically sell their soul for a piece of bread.

I have watched people vote for politicians who favor and promote homosexuality, abortion and other sins in direct violation to the Word of God. Some Christians vote for these candidates because they offer some kind of financial incentive. The Bible very boldly calls it what it is: The spirit of Balaam.

This evil spirit is a spirit of gain or the "What's-in-it-for-me" spirit. This spirit blinds our eyes so we cannot see the truth behind it. It appeals to our personal desire to make sure our needs are met no matter the cost. Money will always reveal the true heart of a person.

Some of you probably thought that I was going to reprimand preachers who are in the ministry for money. But the problem we face is not just with ministers—it is a national problem. The problem is a demon spirit that will deceive us because we, like Balaam, think God must be in favor of any scheme that will make our lives easier or our checkbooks fatter.

This is the hour that we, as children of God and members of the Church, must put our trust in God and not in man. God has given us a means of securing our future and it is called the tithe. *Now, do not shut this*

1. Barna Research Group, Ltd. "Practical Outcomes Replace Biblical Principles as the Moral Standard." *The Barna Update.* Copyright September 10, 2001. Date accessed: October 20, 2003. <http://www.barna.org/cgi-bin/PagePressRelease.asp?PressReleaseID=97&Reference=D.>

book. You have read it this far; you need to hear what the Spirit of God is saying to His Church. God's Word is true and the majority of God's people live in financial bondage because they do not do what He has commanded them to do.

People have no right to exercise a voice in their local church unless they are tithers. Until they decide to obey the Word and tithe, they need to just sit there, be quiet and listen. Non-tithers end up big losers. They lose out on the opportunity to have God bless them financially.

When we hold back what belongs to God, it shuts the windows of heaven over our lives. Malachi 3:8 says, "Will a man rob God?" You ask how can anyone take something from God? The truth is no one can. What we do when we do not tithe is rob God of the blessing and right for Him to bless *us.* We keep Him from doing what He wants to do in our lives, which is to prosper us and get involved in our finances.

I have seen God change people's financial problems when they made the decision to tithe. Our tithe, which is the first 10 percent of our income, is the key to opening the windows of heaven over our lives. If we had a key to a door and we knew great abundance was behind that door, what would we do? We would simply use the key to unlock the door, open it and enjoy the wealth.

Well, our tithes and offerings are the keys to unlock the doors of blessing in our lives—but only 12 percent of the Body of Christ currently accesses that blessing.[2] Of course, the purpose of the tithe is for our local church to have the financial resources to do what God has called it to do. That is why it is so important for God's people to tithe. Without the tithe the local church is hindered.

I remember an incident while I was attending college, working for a valet parking service. Although I parked cars for several restaurants, my only income was from the tips I received.

2. Barna Research Group Ltd. "Churches Lose Financial Ground in 2000." *The Barna Update.* Copyright June 5, 2001. Date accessed: October 20.2003. <http://www.barna.org/cgi-bin/PagePressRelease. asp?PressReleaseID=91&Reference-B.>

One night I brought a gentleman's car to the door for him and his wife. Although I had opened the door for his wife, she stood outside the car and watched to see what kind of tip her husband was going to give me. He handed me a quarter.

Now to be real honest, that was an insult to me. I cannot explain why I did this, but I impulsively stuck the quarter over my eye and stood there looking like a pirate. Well, his wife saw it and began to laugh. Although her husband had already gotten in the car she made him get back out. When he did, she berated him for being so cheap and forced him to give me several dollars. I just stood there through this scene and smiled at him. He didn't smile back.

We do the same thing to God. We throw Him a cheap tip every now and then and expect His best to be given to us in return. It is an insult to Him. His best will come to your life when you give Him your best. Best is always relevant.

Where are you right now in your life? What do you have in your possession that is valuable to you? When you give your best to God, He turns and gives His best to you.

We must examine our motives to keep our hearts pure before the Lord. If we allow our decisions to be determined by gain, then we follow after the spirit of Balaam. It is time to tithe and support the work of God in the local church, which will break the power of the spirit of Balaam.

The children of Israel also killed with the sword Balaam the son of Beor,
the soothsayer, among those who were killed by them (Joshua 13:22).

Balaam was a prophet seeking God for the right direction, but when greed and gain became his motive, he began following the leading of a devilish spirit. Consequently, his life was taken from him. We will also lose in the end if we compromise our principles for material gain.

THE REBELLION OF KORAH

Numbers 16 relates the story of Korah, who instigated a rebellion against Moses and Aaron. He, along with 250 of Israel's chief princes, wanted more authority in the congregation, while charging Moses and Aaron had too much.

These rebels brought eight accusations against Moses. They claimed Moses and Aaron:

• Exercised more authority than they had the right to.

• Thought they were holy.

• Lifted themselves up above the other people.

• Brought them out of Egypt, the real land of milk and honey, to let them die in the wilderness.

• Made themselves princes over the people.

• Did not bring them into the promise land.

• Did not give the people an inheritance of fields and vineyards as promised.

• Blinded the eyes of the people to the fact that none of these promises had been kept.

Every accusation Korah and his followers made exposed their own motives. These were transgressions of which they were guilty.

Therefore you are inexcusable, O man, whoever you are who judge, for in whatever you judge another you condemn yourself; for you who judge practice the same things (Romans 2:1).

If you look closely, you can clearly see the same spirit of rebellion is alive and in full force today. It is a spirit that challenges Christian leadership. We can put those same accusations in a modern context. The pastor is often accused of:

• Having too much authority.

• Thinking he is the only one who can hear from God.

• Exalting himself above the people.

• Not leading the church in the right direction.

• Acting like a king over people who pay his salary.

• Teaching things that apply to him, but not to us.

• Preaching about the promises of God, but those promises are not being fulfilled.

• Not teaching the whole truth.

We must consider the source of this attitude; it is the spirit of Korah. It is a rebellious, independent, prideful and antichrist spirit. This spirit refuses to submit to any authority and challenges all spiritual authority.

No one can grant a position of spiritual authority—neither can it be earned. It can only come from God and God alone. No one is born with it, nor is it imparted by the laying on of hands. God bestows it by His divine touch.

Have you ever been around a godly person and when he or she speaks, everyone gets quiet to listen? That is a demonstration of spiritual authority given by God. These individuals have the spiritual authority to bring closure to a situation due to the wisdom they possess.

God has given our pastors a place of spiritual authority in the local church. The office they hold has been designated as that of God's spokesperson. The pastor is to reveal the Lord's strategy for the local body of believers and the Body of Christ. There is a difference between the shepherd and the sheep. Shepherds are called to lead God's people as well as protect them from the encroachment of the enemy. God has placed them in the Body to watch over your souls. It is for your own protection that you allow them to serve you in this way. Do not be afraid to follow them because their heart and gift is to lead you to safe pastures. If you reject their ministry, then you are left on your own without that support and protection.

And I will give you shepherds according to My heart, who will feed you with knowledge and understanding (Jeremiah 3:15).

Here is a very important component to a victorious Christian life, as well as to world evangelism. The Hebrew word for *knowledge* in this Scripture is *de'ah*, which is used only six times in the entire Bible. This word is described as the *divine knowledge of God*. According to this Scripture, the *pastor imparts* to his people this kind of divine knowledge.

The same word for knowledge is used in Isaiah 11:9:

They shall not hurt nor destroy in all My holy mountain, for the earth shall be full of the knowledge of the Lord as the waters cover the sea (Isaiah 11:9).

It is the type of knowledge that covers the earth, as the waters cover the sea. Could it be that God will use the local church to spread this divine knowledge throughout the earth? If so—according to Jeremiah 3:15—shouldn't we be seeking the knowledge that our pastor can impart to us?

In addition to the knowledge of God, pastors also impart *understanding* which means "to be prudent, circumspect, to wisely understand and to prosper." Pastors fashioned after God's own heart will impart understanding that:

• Encourages clear, biblical thinking (Deuteronomy 32:29).

• Equips us for ministry by imparting understanding and instruction that comes from the Spirit of God (Nehemiah 9:20).

• Instructs us in order that we can be guided by Him (Psalm 32:8).

• Invigorates our hunger for God (Psalm 14:2).

• Keeps us from hell (Proverbs 15:24).

• Brings us happiness (Proverbs 16:20).

• Makes us wise in our instruction to others (Proverbs 16:23).

• Aids us in training our children (Proverbs 17:2).

A pastor fashioned after God's own heart is the original "gift" that keeps on giving. A pastor should be precious in the sight of the believer who understands the valuable instruction he or she offers. As ministers of God, their wisdom originates from God's throne, and whatever we apply that godly wisdom to will prosper.

In the Body of Christ there are three kinds of people: Sheep, goats and wolves. The sheep can be ministered to, the goats butt or challenge everything and the wolf is out to devour the sheep. He is sent by the devil to destroy the flock.

When people open themselves up to a wrong spirit and begin to speak against the authority of the local church, they conform to the spirit of Korah. I have seen this spirit arise in associate ministers and key leaders in the church on countless occasions. I have counseled with many pastors who are going through such situations.

The end result is destruction. The ground swallowed Korah. Moses did not have to defend himself at all. God had already judged rebellion, and destruction was its reward.

I had a student come to Bible school one year who challenged everything. At the beginning of the year in my initial interview with him, he told me the guidelines we had in place were different from the school he had just left. I did not respond to this statement at first, but when he said it for the third time I could not ignore it.

I shared with him what I thought would be a revelation that might help him. I told him he was not at the previous school any longer, he was here now and this is the way we operated our school. My position was either ignored or misunderstood because this same young man went on to cause problems, not only in the school, but everywhere he went because of the attitude of rebellion in his life. He would not receive correction, so I was unable to help him.

On another occasion, while taking a test a student told me that he would answer the questions, not from the information that had been taught, but according to what he thought was right. When I explained he would be dismissed from school if he failed the first eight weeks of class, he was very angry. Just a few days later I was forced to dismiss him from the school—and he left calling the fire of God down on me. (Now that will really make your day.)

You may be asking yourself why I didn't cast the devil out of him. I had attempted to minister to him on several occasions, but he would not receive ministry. You cannot help people if they do not want your help. He was a wolf in sheep's clothing.

A wolf will always come in looking and acting like a sheep. These impostors are always the most spiritual people you have ever met. They have more spiritual visions and dreams than everyone else. They often tell you about Jesus manifesting in the flesh to talk to them. In fact, from the way they talk, you would think they see Jesus more than the Father sees Him! Eventually they show their true character when they begin to speak against the authority of the local church.

Once I was counseling a person, trying to minister correction to him because of all the strife he was causing in the church he attended. However, every time I would speak, he would tell me about how Jesus appeared to him in his bedroom. Jesus had given him specific instructions and, oddly enough, it was directly opposite of what I was telling him.

After this had continued quite a while, I told him that he had convinced me of one thing—Jesus the Messiah, the Son of God had moved His residence from the right hand of the Father and was now living in his bedroom.

He didn't like that very much. I may not have been as tactful as I could have been; however, I was trying to help him. I was trying to get him to realize that his actions were causing strife and division in the church and were not done under the direction of the Lord.

But if you have bitter envy and self-seeking in your hearts, do not boast and lie against the truth. This wisdom does not descend from above, but is earthly, sensual, demonic. For where envy and self-seeking exist, confusion and every evil thing are there (James 3:14–16).

The spirit of Korah will always manifest itself in strife, selfishness and envy. *The manifesting fruit shows where it originates.* Always remember that strife is the manifested presence of the devil.

When he hears the cry of the wolf, a true present-day shepherd will not go and get a rod or staff. He will get a 30-30 rifle and go after the wolf for the sake of the flock! Do not stand in judgment of your pastor when he uses his spiritual authority to correct people causing strife.

Cast out the scoffer, and contention will leave; yes, strife and reproach will cease (Proverbs 22:10).

Spiritual shepherds will have to deal with wolves in the local church. They must confront them and send them on their way. We in the local church should not judge how the pastor deals with them; we usually do not know the entire situation. We must stay away from those who cause strife, because they will bring the presence of the devil right into our homes.

In Matthew 21 the Bible says Jesus, full of zeal, watched the temple being misused and dishonored. So He made a whip and went after the offenders with the intention of causing pain. He literally beat those men out of the temple that day.

Imagine if your pastor acted like Jesus in this story, while you were a door greeter trying to make visitors feel welcome. I can just picture it. "Welcome to our church. Here comes our pastor now." Then the pastor rushes past you and the visitor with a whip in his hand, chasing someone out of the church!

If we could go back in time and watch that episode of Jesus at the temple take place, I wonder how we would judge it. We might say, "Well that's not a man of love!"

Sure Jesus was a man of love—I believe he *loved* every minute of it (just joking, I know that He didn't). But the power of His love for His Father overwhelmed Him as He observed this tragic abuse of His Father's house and quickly responded to correct this exploitation of God's people.

The point is we don't have the right to judge our pastor in a similar situation. We usually don't know the whole story. A wolf has to be driven out in order for the sheep to be safe. Let the leaders do what they are called to do—feed and protect the flock.

IF JESUS CAN SUBMIT, YOU CAN TOO

There is a revelation that has been a real eye-opener for me. During my years as associate pastor, this understanding helped me work with my senior pastor, and it has helped me submit in the difficult times of my own personal life.

> *His parents went to Jerusalem every year at the Feast of the Passover. And when He was twelve years old, they went up to Jerusalem according to the custom of the feast. When they had finished the days, as they returned, the Boy Jesus lingered behind in Jerusalem. And Joseph and His mother did not know it; but supposing Him to have been in the company, they went a day's journey, and sought Him among their relatives and acquaintances. So when they did not find Him, they returned to Jerusalem, seeking Him. Now so it was that after three days they found Him in the temple, sitting in the midst of the teachers, both listening to them and asking them questions. And all who heard Him were astonished at His understanding and answers. So when they saw Him, they were amazed; and His mother said*

to Him, "Son, why have You done this to us? Look, Your father and I have sought You anxiously" (Luke 2:41-48).

The Message translation says, "Your father and I have been half out of our minds looking for you!"

To understand this important principle, we can imagine a similar situation in our own lives. For instance, let's say you have been traveling for eight hours before stopping for a rest, only to discover your 12-year-old son, who you thought was somewhere in the large group you are traveling with, has apparently been left behind. What would your reaction be?

As a Christian, you probably would begin to pray and plead the blood of Jesus over his life, and then you would call 9-1-1. After the initial panic subsides you would think, "If that child was not paying attention and missed the trip because he was playing around, he is grounded until he's 40."

Now try to picture how Mary, the mother of Jesus, must have felt. Let's face it, she probably thought, *Dear Lord, I gave birth to the Son of God and now I've lost Him.*

It was three days before they found Jesus in the temple. Now I know how moms are—Mary had not slept or eaten for 72 hours. She was emotionally and physically worn out. She must have been just like any other mom who has lost her child. After all those days and all that worry, they find that He is in the temple having the time of His life. She must have said something to Him like, "Jesus, You have driven me out of my mind. What were You thinking?"

Jesus responded in verse 49, "Why did you seek Me? Did you not know that I must be about My Father's business?" While this statement may give the impression that Jesus was being a little smart with His mother, we know He wasn't. He was being honest, but He could have gotten just a little ahead of God's perfect timing. Don't forget He was only twelve years old.

The Scriptures do not tell us how Mary responded to Jesus after this answer. We can only imagine what was going through her mind after three days of no sleep. However, we do know that Jesus did find the wonderful place of balance between the will of His Father and His place as Mary's son because as we go down to verse 51 we discover that He *subjected* His life to them.

> *Then He went down with them and came to Nazareth, and was **subject** to them, but His mother kept all these things in her heart* (emphasis added.)

People wonder what Jesus did from the time He was 12 to the time He was 30. Well, wonder no more. He did *everything* His earthly parents *told* Him to do. When I read that Scripture, the Lord said to me, "Terry, if I, as the Son of God, can submit Myself to human flesh for 18 years, then you can submit in any situation you face." I had to do some repenting at that moment.

It could not have been easy for Jesus to submit all the time. He was a normal kid. He had to make a decision to submit to His parent's authority as the Word of God taught. I am sure Jesus occasionally had babysitting duty, because the oldest brother always has more responsibility than the other children. If He was subject to them, He did it without complaining.

There were probably times when one of the younger brothers needed a clean diaper and Mary asked Jesus to change him. He could have said, "Wait just a minute, I am the Lord God and I change not!" His refusal would have been technically in line with the Word of God. But Jesus obeyed and submitted to His parents.

There is compensation and reward for laying down your own desires to fulfill someone else's. While I was reading this, I asked the Holy Spirit, "What do I get in return for choosing to flow with authority and following orders?"

He told me to keep reading.

*And Jesus increased in **wisdom** and **stature**, and in **favor** with God and men* (Luke 2:52, emphasis added).

So, this is what we get when we submit: *Wisdom, stature* and *favor* with God and man.

I am not advocating unconditional submission. If someone asks us to do something that violates the Scriptures, we have a higher authority to answer to, which is the Word of God.

But the truth is, usually this is not the case. Some people struggle when it comes to submitting to the straightforward rules of the church nursery. However, when you determine in your heart that you are going to flow with the spiritual authority in your life, you open the door for the favor of God to manifest.

As we are careful to guard ourselves from the way of Cain, the error of Balaam and the rebellion of Korah, we will walk in the maturity of God and be overcomers in these last days.

When we get out of our comfort zone, develop the gift zone and face the challenge zone, we will be ready to run into the end zone.

THE END ZONE

Running into the end zone is the goal of every NFL football player. Scoring is the reason they are playing the game. They are there to win.

When the goal line is crossed, a sense of victory rises in the heart of the player. I believe God intends for all His children to cross the finish line. *The end zone is the place of victory.*

Maurice Green, U.S. gold medal winner of the 100-meter dash in the 2000 Olympics, is known as the fastest man in the world. When the U.S. track team was preparing for the relay race, the coaches placed Maurice on the last leg.

It is important how you start, but it is more important how you finish. The coaches took the second fastest man and put him in the first leg of the race. They positioned the third fastest runner in the second leg, and the fourth fastest in the third leg of the race just before Maurice.

When the gun sounded, the first runner raced to his teammate and handed off the baton. The second runner continued the race, handing off the baton to the third runner. The third runner handed the baton to Maurice to finish the race. He put all his energy and determination into his race and the team won the gold medal.

I believe when Jesus handed off the baton of Christianity, He handed it to those who were the second fastest runners. These men ran their leg of the race and handed the baton off to the next generation. It has been handed down from generation to generation until it has reached us—who I believe are the last generation. *I believe Jesus sees us as the fastest runners.* We are the ones destined, chosen, literally handpicked by God to finish this race.

Several years ago I ran a marathon, which is 26.2 miles. As I ran past the 25-mile mark, I began to rejoice in my heart because I knew I had just one mile to go. My legs had started to cramp, but in my heart I was determined to finish the race. Nearing the end I looked up and saw a beautiful sight. Stretched across the road in big bold letters were the words, "FINISH LINE."

I was running with a small group of people, and the sight of that sign revitalized us. We picked up speed as we raced toward that line and completely forgot about the pain we were experiencing. A sudden burst of energy from somewhere deep inside drove us on past the finish line. It was that burst of energy—and the cheering, picture-taking crowd we wanted to impress—that propelled us to victory.

This is comparable to our spiritual race. There is a power within us, originating from the Holy Ghost that propels us across the finish line. We, as one of the last generations called by God to finish this spiritual race, are the fastest runners. God has saved the best for last.

When Jesus turned the water into wine, the wedding guests came to the governor of the feast and said, "You have saved the best for last." This is a spiritual principle, proving the best is yet to come.

God chose *us* to labor in these endtimes. He has put within us a new spirit of victory. We can be all God has called us to be.

Victory is in you. Romans 16:20a says, "And the God of peace will crush Satan under your feet shortly." This makes it clear that God has designed you to crush the enemy. Your gifts and calling will destroy his kingdom, because your gift is designed to bring people into the Kingdom of God.

Rise up by the Spirit of God and go do what God has called you to do. Be like the commercial for athletic shoes and "just do it." Get plugged into your local church, be faithful, run your race and *win*.

GET IN THE GAME

Seeing players cross the goal line inspires others to get into the game. How many children are playing golf today because they have watched Tiger Woods? How many are playing basketball because of Michael Jordan's fame? When we watch athletes do what most people think cannot be done, we are inspired.

The end-time Church will inspire the world in a way that has never been seen before. Habakkuk 2:14 promises, "For the earth will be filled with the knowledge of the glory of the Lord, as the waters cover the sea." God's glory is coming upon us and will be seen on us. That visual representation of the Lord will motivate the world to seek God.

The testimony of your Christian walk will inspire this generation for Christ. Hebrews 11:38 says, "the world was not worthy" of the faith-filled men and women of God who, by faith, took kingdoms for God.

There is a new generation being raised up by the Spirit of God who will shake the nations for God's glory, although the world is not worthy of these people. There will be young people with the spirit of David who will proclaim, "You come to me with the sword and spear, but I come in the name of the Lord the God of Israel." There will be senior citizens with the spirit of Caleb who, at 80 years old demanded, "Give me my mountain." God is going to pour out His Spirit on all flesh. This is a new day of God's Spirit.

If we have allowed strife or bitterness to arise between the pastor and ourselves, we must be bold enough to go and put things right. It is too late in the ball game to allow anything to keep us from fulfilling our assignment.

THE GOAL LINE IS THE PLACE WHERE WE DISCOVER IT WAS ALL WORTH IT

Once the clock runs out, the game is over and we stand victorious, we will know that everything we went through to make it this far was worth it.

In Second Kings 2, the Bible tells the story of Elijah and his ascension into Heaven. Elisha, whom some scholars believe served Elijah faithfully between 10 and 20 years, was right there with him.

In verses 3 and 5, the sons of the prophets came to Elisha and asked him, "Do you know that the Lord will take away your master from over you today?" Elisha answered, "I know it but hold your peace."

They were trying to get Elisha to leave his post. *It will not be the sinner who tries to talk us out of being faithful to our calling—it will be Christian brothers and sisters.*

Several years ago, I was ministering at church one Sunday morning and after the service, a young man walked up to me and said, "Thus saith the Lord, Brother Terry—you need to be in your own ministry."

I immediately replied, "Thus saith Brother Terry, I am already in my own ministry."

At the time, I was doing exactly what God had called me to do. Each of us must know in our hearts what God has told us and stick with it. Do not listen to the voices of those telling you how great your ministry is and that you need to be in your own ministry when you know it is not your time yet.

My pastor once told me, "If someone prophesies that you are to go to Africa, then you better take them with you so you will know when it is time to come home." In other words, *we need to listen to the Holy Spirit and follow His instructions, rather than the words of man*—regardless of good intentions.

Elisha watched Elijah head to Heaven in a chariot of fire, and the mantle of Elijah fell on him that day. He went to the Jordan River and cried out, "Where is the Lord God of Elijah?" and the river parted.

He knew the double portion he had requested was truly his. Once he crossed the river, the sons of the prophets came, knelt before him and recognized that the anointing from Elijah was now upon him. The very ones who tried to talk him out of being faithful were the first ones to recognize the anointing.

If we stay in the place God has led us and are faithful, the very people who try to get us to move ahead of God's timing will be the first to recognize the anointing upon our lives.

The key is to stay put, be faithful and do whatever it takes to finish the game. We will face challenges in life but the Greater One is *in* us, *for* us and *with* us.

We cannot lose.

Chapter 4

It's Time to...
Get Ready to Become a Voice and Not an Echo

A pastor and his wife were driving to a church meeting and decided to stop along the road to rest and stretch their legs. When they got out of their car, they noticed a cemetery across the road. Since the wife enjoyed reading old headstones to see how the deceased were memorialized, they decided to spend a few minutes wandering through the cemetery.

As they walked along, they discovered an epitaph they both felt was the best they had ever read. They would never forget it.

It said:

> *EVERYTHING I SPENT IN LIFE I HAVE LOST*
> *EVERYTHING I GAINED IN LIFE I NOW GIVE*
> *TO SOMEONE ELSE*
> *THE ONLY THING I TAKE WITH ME*
> *IS WHAT I HAVE GIVEN AWAY*

❦❦❦❦❦❦❦❦

WE MUST BE RICH IN GOOD WORKS

And behold, I am coming quickly, and My reward is with Me, to give to every one according to his work (Revelation 22:12).

The word *reward* means "to pay for service." The word *work* refers to "acts or deeds."

Are you ready to meet Jesus? Most everyone would say, "Yes! I can't wait to see Him."

But are you ready to be judged by Him? Are you ready to receive the payment for your service? Do you realize that before we enter into Heaven, we must go before the Judgment Seat of Christ and give account of the works we have done on the earth?

> *For we must all appear and be revealed as we are before the judgment seat of Christ, so that each one may receive [his pay] according to what he has done in the body, whether good or evil [considering what his purpose and motive have been, and what he has achieved, been busy with, and given himself and his attention to accomplishing]* (2 Corinthians 5:10 AMP).

Our families will not be there to say we were good parents or sons or daughters. Our pastor will not be sending a recommendation letter. We will stand there before Jesus alone and He will judge us according to what we did on earth for Him.

What we do on this earth for Jesus will determine our rank and position in Heaven. The Bible tells us that we shall reign as kings and priests. I believe Jesus will assign positions to those who have used their abilities and talents for the Kingdom of God and not their own interests.

> *Now if anyone builds on this foundation with gold, silver, precious stones, wood, hay, straw, each one's work will become clear; for the Day will declare it, because it will be revealed by fire; and the fire will test each one's work, of what sort it is. If anyone's work which he has built on it endures, he will receive a reward. If anyone's work is burned, he will suffer loss; but he himself will be saved, yet so as through fire* (1 Corinthians 3:12–15).

According to Strong's Concordance, the word *fire* used here means "fiery fire."

I was praying about this one day and I asked the Lord to help me understand how our works will be tried. Will it be literal fire from Heaven that will come down and consume those works not of God, or will it be something else? I began searching the Scriptures and found that the word *fire* in this passage is the same word used in Revelation 1:14 when John saw Jesus.

> *And in the midst of the seven lampstands One like the Son of Man, clothed with a garment down to the feet and girded about the chest with a golden band. His head and hair were white like wool, as white as snow,* ***and His eyes like a flame of fire****; His feet were like fine brass, as if refined in a furnace, and His voice as the sound of many waters* (Revelation 1:13-15, emphasis added).

John describes Jesus' eyes as a "*flame of fire*" or fiery fire. I believe this is how Jesus will judge our works. We will stand before Him and look at our works as something to be proud of; but when Jesus looks at them through His eyes of fire, they will be seen in their purest form. I believe the fire in His eyes will judge the motive of every work.

If we accomplish what He asked of us, it is as gold, silver and precious stones. If what we accomplished was done for selfish gain, it will dissolve before us and there will be no reward.

How Jesus views things is undoubtedly different from how we view the same things. Jesus will look at our works and the fire in His eyes will try them. It is His Word that judges the intents of our heart.

> *For the word of God is living and powerful, and sharper than any two-edged sword, piercing even to the division of soul and spirit, and of joints and marrow, and is a discerner of the thoughts and intents of the heart* (Hebrews 4:12).

The Amplified Version says, "*exposing and sifting and analyzing and judging the very thoughts and purposes of the heart.*" It goes on to say that nothing goes unseen by Him.

> *And there is no creature hidden from His sight, but all things are naked and open to the eyes of Him to whom we must give account* (Hebrews 4:13).

We cannot hide our true motives from the Lord.

WHEN YOU DO IT TO THEM, YOU DO IT TO HIM

One hot summer day I was told of a church member who did not have air conditioning in her car. She had been without it for two years because she did not have the money to fix it, which would have required installing an entirely new air conditioning unit.

When I went home that day I told my wife, Kim, about the situation. Immediately she said, "I'll fix it."

The instant she said it, I heard the Lord speak to my heart, "Kim just fixed the air conditioning in *My* car."

I stopped and said to the Lord, "No! She just fixed the air conditioning for this family."

Then this Scripture came to me.

*Then the righteous will answer Him, saying, "Lord, when did we see You hungry and feed You, or thirsty and give You drink? When did we see You a stranger and take You in, or naked and clothe You? Or when did we see You sick, or in prison, and come to You?" And the King will answer and say to them, "Assuredly, I say to you, **inasmuch as you did it to one of the least of these My brethren, you did it to Me**"* (Matthew 25:37-40, emphasis added).

When Kim stands before the Lord, He will say to her, "Do you remember when I did not have air conditioening in My car?"

She may answer, "When was that Lord?"

The Lord will reply, "When you did it for *them*, you did it for *Me*." The Lord will then command the angels to bring her reward. That is exactly how it is going to work when we stand before Him.

When I was young we used to sing the song, "When We All Get to Heaven." I remember the words, "When we all get to heaven, what a day of rejoicing that will be! When we all see Jesus, we will sing and shout the victory."

Now, it *will* be great to see Him. But again, are we ready to be judged by Him? Some will not be shouting the victory, because there will be no reward given to them for the work they did on earth.

When Jesus visited the seven churches in the Book of Revelation, each time He said to them, "I know your works" (see Rev. 2–3).

He did not say, "I know your *faith*"; He said, "I know your *works*."

James, the brother of Jesus, put it this way in his letter to the Diaspora (dispersed tribes of Israel):

For as the body without the spirit is dead, so faith without works is dead also (James 2:26).

Jesus is looking at our works. When He returns, I will stand before Him and He will ask me, "Terry, what did you do with the gifts and talents that I gave you in the earth?" I will be judged as a steward over the works He gave me to do.

GOD SOWS THE GIFTS, WE GROW THE GIFTS

One morning as I was meditating on Revelation 22:12, I asked the Lord to prepare me for the Judgment Seat of Christ. I told the Lord that I didn't want to treat the ministry like a job. I did not want to visit the sick because it is what I am paid to do. I did not want to counsel people and pray for people because it is my profession. I thought about the things I used to do for the Lord without receiving any compensation. I was very honest with Him that day. I truly want to stand before Him and hear Him say, "Well done."

A few weeks later, I had an opportunity to see if I meant that prayer. I left the house to pick up a few things at the store. On the way home, I noticed my gas tank was nearly empty. (My wife does not have the gift of filling up the car.)

It was raining and I was in a hurry. I was getting a little irritated and I did not want to get out of the car because of the rain. However, I stopped at a gas station near my home and quickly started filling the tank, trying not to get wet.

Suddenly someone tapped me on the shoulder. I turned to find a young lady, probably in her mid-teens, soaking wet and crying. She looked up at me and asked if I would give her a ride to the grocery store, a couple of miles down the road.

She explained that she was from out of town, but was staying with friends. She had walked two miles to this gas station to get milk for her friend's baby. She told me she only had six dollars worth of food stamps, however the gas station would not accept them. She had asked several other people to help her, but they all had ignored her.

I told her that I would be glad to drive her to the store. I knew in my spirit that the Lord was giving me this opportunity to witness.

On the way to the store, I began telling her about Jesus. She told me how she had known the Lord at one time but had fallen away from Him. She had the same denominational background that I did, so it was easy for me to identify with her. I ministered to her about the love of God, that Jesus had a purpose for her life and that it was not an accident she had asked me to help her.

When we arrived at the grocery store, I knew in my spirit exactly what I was supposed to do. I turned off the car and said to her, "Let's go. I am buying your groceries."

Needless to say, she was shocked! She could not believe that I was going to do this. She kept asking me, "Why?" I told her not to worry about it. I grabbed a cart and said, "Now just tell me what you want."

As we went down the cereal aisle, she was still so shocked and embarrassed that she took her finger, put it next to her face and pointed but did not say a word. I asked her if she wanted the Cheerios that she seemed to be indicating. She nodded; so I asked which she wanted—honey, plain or frosted. She said the plain would be fine. I put several boxes in the cart and again I told her, "*All you have to do is just tell me what you want!*"

Next we went to the meat department and I asked her if she needed some meat. She responded in an embarrassed way. So I asked her if she wanted chicken, beef, pork or any other kind of meat. I made it clear to her again that all she had to do was to tell me what she wanted. She again pointed with a finger next to her face, revealing her embarrassment. I put a little of everything in the shopping cart.

We went down each aisle the same way. When we made it to the checkout counter, I will never forget what she asked me. She looked up at me and asked, "Do you want my food stamps?" I laughed and told her I didn't need her food stamps.

After loading the groceries in the car, I asked her, "Do you know why I did this for you?"

She replied, "Was it because you felt sorry for me?"

I told her that it had nothing to do with pity; it was the compassion of God. I shared with her that the Lord loved her and had a plan for her life. I drove her to the apartment where she was staying, all the while telling her of the love of God.

After letting her out and helping her with the groceries, I prayed for her. As I was driving home, the Lord spoke to me. He said, "I am going to share with you two lessons that I want you to remember. The first is that the Church is too much like that girl in the grocery store. I have provided for them all they will ever need and desire, but they look at the provisions and say, 'Just give me a little of that.' It's like they look at Me and ask Me if I want their food stamps. All I want is for them to believe Me and ask Me for what they want."

GOD'S NOT CHEAP

I remember one Christmas looking at all the presents under the Christmas tree and telling my wife, "There is not one present under that tree that our children need."

My children never ask me for what they need; they always ask me for what they want. My oldest daughter, to this day, petitions me for the things she wants. She will get the magazines out and show me pictures of the items she desires and then share with me the amount of money that I need to believe God for. She is totally convinced that her dad will take care of it for her and do all he can do to fulfill her desires.

If God only supplies our needs, then I, in the natural, am a better father than Him. Thank God that isn't true! The Word tells us that He provides for more than our needs.

If you then, being evil, know how to give good gifts to your children, how much more will your Father who is in heaven give good things to those who ask Him! (Matthew 7:11).

...you do not have because you do not ask (James 4:2).

I grew up in a small town in Arkansas, where my dad owned a shoe store called, The Shoe Box. I have a twin brother and we are the babies of the family. If you know anything about the babies of the family, you know they have special privileges.

My twin brother and I went off to college and I fondly recall the times we would return home to visit our parents. One of the first things we would do is get the key to the shoe store. We would not go during the day; we would go there at night. We made sure the store was empty. Then we would lock the door behind us and help ourselves to what we called "the five-finger discount." That means getting all we could carry and, if necessary, making two trips.

When we would come home, my dad would look at all the shoes we carried and say, "You guys never get the cheap stuff."

We would always say, "Dad, we're not stupid." We knew where my dad kept the most expensive shoes.

You may be thinking, "Brother Terry, how could you do such a thing?" It's simple: Because MY DAD OWNED THE PLACE!

There are rights and privileges for those whose parents own the place. Now if you tried that in my dad's store, it would be called shoplifting and you would be arrested.

Our heavenly Father owns this planet we live on, and yet we walk and act like we have nothing. Jesus' blood paid the price and made us sons of God. As sons, it is our faith that reaches to God and receives what He has provided for us.

START WHERE YOU ARE

There was something else the Lord revealed to me the day I bought those groceries. I had taken the young lady *to* the grocery store because she had *asked* me to. However, when I took her *into* the store and *bought* her groceries, those deeds were placed into my heavenly account because I *chose* to do those things.

When we go the extra mile for someone and we do it as unto the Lord, it is added to our account in Heaven.

In Matthew 25, Jesus gave talents to three servants before leaving on a trip. In verse 19, the Bible says He returned to settle the accounts with them. I believe we have heavenly accounts that we make deposits into every day by our good works. When we are asked to help in the church and we determine to do a good job as unto the Lord, rewards are then set up for us in Heaven.

When someone is sick and we visit them and give of ourselves by cooking a meal for them, we lay up rewards in our heavenly account. When we are always on time for the positions we hold in the church and we honor God with those positions, I believe rewards are laid up in Heaven.

Whenever we do things for the Lord's sake, and not to impress others, we lay up treasures in Heaven.

> *For the kingdom of heaven is like a man traveling to a far country, who called his own servants and delivered **his goods** to them* (Matthew 25:14, emphasis added).

The Amplified Bible says the goods we receive from the Lord are "entrusted" goods. They do not belong to us. The talents we possess are not ours; they have been entrusted to us. We cannot claim this ability on our own. It has merely been loaned to us, and we will give account to Jesus for it. It is His and He loaned it to us, to go out and increase it. What we do with it and how we use it is up to us. God sows the gifts to us, but we are responsible to grow the gifts.

Jesus gave talents to His servants and then He returned to collect on what He had given. The one who had received five talents traded and used his wisely, gaining five more to equal ten. He received his reward from the master.

> *His lord said to him, "Well done, good and faithful servant...*(Matthew 25:21).

Notice that Jesus judged the *character* of the man and not the *production* of the man. It is not the amount that God looks for in us, but the character of the work and our faithfulness to Him. *Who we are* must be the basis for *what we do.* Our actions should originate in a heart that is deeply in love with God. That inward love will be manifested in our outward actions.

> *...you were faithful over a few things, **I will** make you ruler over many things. Enter into the joy of your lord* (Matthew 25:21, emphasis added).

Praise God! The slave just became a ruler. When we are faithful to use what we have been given, God blesses us. The key is to start with what we have been given and then be faithful with it. We don't need to look at someone else and wish we had his or her talent. We just need to open our eyes and start where we are.

For I was hungry and you gave Me food; I was thirsty and you gave Me drink; I was a stranger and you took Me in (Matthew 25:35).

You don't need a degree to operate in good works. Just start doing something! Why not look around and find a family who is hungry and give them some food? God is not asking you to sing to them, just feed them! They don't want to hear you sing when they need something in their stomachs. Jesus said, "I was hungry and you gave Me food."

All you need to do is find someone thirsty and help provide the water to quench their thirst. That could apply in many areas of a person's life. Again, God is simply asking us to use what we already have. I may not be able to give the thirsty man a million dollars, but I can get him a glass of water. I cannot give what I do not have. God only expects me to give out of what I have.

I was naked and you clothed Me; I was sick and you visited Me; I was in prison and you came to Me (Matthew 25:36).

What is God commanding us to do? To simply open our eyes to the needs of people and feed them, clothe them, visit them, pray for their healing, and invite them into our homes. He said when we have done it for others, we have done it for Him. This is how we lay up treasures in Heaven. We have to determine to do something for someone else. It is from this action of serving others, that the will of God presents itself to us.

I remember when I first went to work at Agape Church. I met my pastor at the front door on Sunday morning at 9:00 a.m. and we went in and straightened a few chairs. He tested the microphone to make sure it was working properly. He turned on the air conditioning and then said to me, "We are ready for the service."

I then stated, "If you will give me the key to the church, I will take care of these things for you. Pastor, you go get in the Word and prayer and

I will set everything up for the service." He handed me the key and never asked for it back.

I did not need to have three dreams and two visions to get that revelation. I could see the need and knew I could fill it. My call and ministry began right there.

And this is just where yours will begin as well. Stop crying for God to use you and start asking God to give you eyes for the harvest. Often the harvest is right in front of you.

WE MUST BE FERVENT IN PRAYER

As the return of Jesus gets closer and closer, we must be rich in good works and we must be people of prayer.

God is calling the Church into a new level of intercession for an awakening in our nation. The prayers of believers must continually cover our nation. We have within us the power, through prayer, to stop the devil from initiating his destructive work in our country.

We have to realize that we are in a war with the forces of darkness. The only way we are going to be able to combat the forces coming upon the earth in these last days is for the Church to awaken to who they are in Christ and to the power of the Holy Spirit.

The Holy Spirit is yearning to take us to a new level. But we are going to have to become desperate to reach a new level. The people who are desperate will be the ones who reach out for God with all that is within them. They are the ones He will answer.

Some time ago, the Lord spoke to my spirit for several days saying, "The voice of one." I heard this over and over again. I continued working and going through my daily routine, all the while hearing, "The voice of one," over and over for several weeks.

I knew where this phrase was located in the Bible because I had preached on it many times before.

The voice of one crying in the wilderness: "Prepare the way of the Lord; make straight in the desert a highway for our God" (Isaiah 40:3).

Notice it is the voice of one *crying*, not just one making a lot of noise. God knows the difference between noise and the cry of faith. This is someone whose heart is reaching up to touch the power of God.

The woman with the issue of blood began to press through with her faith.

*For she **said**, "If only I may touch His clothes, I shall be made well"* (Mark 5:28, emphasis added).

This woman was desperate. She had been plagued for many years with illness and had lost everything. She was at the bottom of the barrel. Even though she knew she could be stoned for being in a crowd while she had an "issue of blood," she was still desperate for a touch from the Lord. She knew it could cost her everything to press through the crowd. Despite the danger, she put her faith on the line and pressed forward to touch Him.

Then Jesus stopped and asked, "*Who touched My clothes?*"

His disciples were amazed Jesus had asked such a question. Couldn't He see all the people? Did He want them to pinpoint just one person? "You see the multitude thronging You, and You say, 'Who touched Me?' " (Mk. 5:31).

Jesus knew someone had touched Him with the touch of desperation and faith, because life had flowed out of Him. Jesus knows the difference between the noise of self-pity and the cry of faith.

ALEX'S CRY OF FAITH

In 1999, my wife and I adopted a little boy from Romania. We started the process in 1997. It took two years to finalize the adoption and bring our son home.

At the time we started adoption proceedings in 1997, we had a 12-year-old daughter. After making the decision to adopt another child, my wife unexpectedly became pregnant in the spring of 1998. This happened more than a decade after doctors told us it would be medically impossible for us to conceive another child. Despite medical disbelief, our second daughter was born in January of 1999 and our new 10-year-old son arrived from Romania five months later.

I went from raising one child to being the father of three in just a couple months. That is what I call, God doing *"exceeding abundantly above all"* that I could ask or think. I told people at that time, we have two new members in our family and neither one of them speaks English.

Our son's Romanian name is Audi, which we have changed to Alex. Alex was born in a Romanian hospital and was left there until he was two years old. His father was in the military and after divorcing his wife, came to the hospital to get his son. Alex lived with his father and stepmother until he was six years old.

Although he no longer had to stay in the hospital, Alex's life at home was not any more nurturing. His father, an alcoholic, beat him many times until there were places on his head where hair would not grow. Since there was little to eat, his stepmother gave him sugar water much of the time. You can imagine what his teeth were like when He came to live with us.

Fortunately, there was a born-again woman living in their neighborhood who visited the family and invited them to church. The parents refused—but Alex, being five years old at the time, begged to go. He was very persistent, so his father finally let him go. It was in that Romanian church, at the age of six, that Alex gave his life to Jesus.

After being born again, Alex prayed for his family, but they still refused to have anything to do with the church. The abuse from his father worsened. After Alex had been beaten to the point of death by his father, the State finally intervened and placed him in an orphanage.

While at the orphanage, Alex prayed and asked Jesus to give him Christian parents from America. The people at the orphanage told him to stop praying because that would never happen. But Alex refused to listen; instead he told them that Jesus would hear his prayer and would answer him.

My wife's aunt, Sue Whiteley, a missionary in Romania, works with several orphanages. One day as she was going about her usual activities, the Holy Spirit abruptly changed her plans. She felt impressed of the Lord to go by and see this particular orphanage where Alex lived. Arriving at the orphanage she spoke to the administration, offering them assistance with food and gifts for the children.

As she visited with the administrative officials in a courtyard area, one of the children told Alex that an American woman was outside. He had never seen an American before, but he had been praying for an American family—so he ran as hard and fast as he could to the courtyard.

Unable to speak English, he simply grabbed Sue's dress and pulled her down to him. She looked at him and said, "You look just like my grandson." The Holy Spirit put something in her heart for him, and she began to come to get him on weekends.

Several months later, Sue contacted us to see if we would consider adopting Alex. Now my first response was, "No way!" I was too busy doing all the work we had here in the ministry and I had too much going on. Besides, my philosophy was built on Psalm 127:4-5, "Like arrows in the hand of a warrior, so are the children of one's youth. Happy is the man who has his quiver full of them; they shall not be ashamed." And I quivered at one child.

It took awhile, but one night the Lord spoke to my spirit very distinctly after my wife returned from a trip to Romania. She had shared with our church; and as I sat there listening, I began to think about the children. I went home that night and began to pray.

The Lord reminded me of all the nations where I have had the privilege of ministering. In my mind, I went back to the times I had ministered in thirdworld nations, with children sitting on the floor all around me as I spoke.

Suddenly I saw myself as a six-year-old boy, sitting in the middle of the floor with all the other poverty-stricken children. When I saw that, I began to weep. I heard the Lord ask, "How far would you want someone to go to get you?"

I immediately got off the bed and said, "Lord, You want me to adopt this child!"

God did one miracle after another to get Alex here to the United States. On May 18, 1999, the very day our INS approval expired, Alex arrived in Little Rock.

Now does God favor one orphan over another? No, of course not. Does God love Alex more than the other children in the orphanage of 200 boys? No, of course not. But God does favor faith and the cry of His children. When a voice rises up and cries out in faith from a heart of desperation, God will hear and He will always answer.

ARE YOU CRYING OR MOANING

The question is—are you pulling on God? God loves us all; but the people who pull on Him will get His attention.

Jesus said to the woman with the issue of blood, "Daughter, your faith has made you well. Go in peace, and be healed of your affliction" (Mk. 5:34).

There is a living faith on the inside of you that is crying to reach up and touch a living God. Not a noise, but the cry of faith—a prayer of faith.

And she was in bitterness of soul, and prayed to the Lord, and wept in anguish (1 Samuel 1:10).

When Hannah cried in faith, praying with all her heart before the Lord, He heard her. As a result of her faith-filled cry, one of the greatest prophets to ever live was born. Hannah was desperate. When you get desperate, you will fervently and earnestly seek God in prayer—and you will get answers.

Daniel was a man motivated by time. In Daniel 9, he began to under-stand that it was time for the children of Israel to come out from Babylonian captivity. He had read the prophecies of Jeremiah, which stat-ed that Israel would be free after 70 years.

As he read, realizing the 70 years were almost up, his spirit began to cry out to God. It did not matter how things looked in the natural. He set himself to pray for God to do what He had promised to do. He fought in prayer against the spirit of Persia. He overcame by persisting in prayer and not quitting.

Daniel's experience teaches a lesson. Just because something has been promised and prophesied, it is still our responsibility to birth it through prayer and intercession.

I believe God is awakening the Church to realize the shortness of time. As this happens, you are going to sense the need to pray, as you have never prayed before, for a move of God in your church and city. There is going to be warfare like you have never experienced, but God is going to see you through it. He will give you the grace to birth the new move of His pres-ence in the earth.

BE A VOICE, NOT AN ECHO

Isaiah 40 says there is a voice that is crying in the wilderness. There are three kinds of wildernesses. The first is a wilderness that you have created yourself through making wrong decisions. It could be a financial decision that has brought you into a wilderness. It could be a decision in your mar-riage or family that you should have never made.

The second wilderness is an attack of the enemy that suddenly comes on you. It could be a sickness that has the ability to take your life and fear has gripped you. The devil has come against you and in the natural you are not going to make it.

The third is a wilderness that is aroused by what is happening around you. Your eyes are opened to something you have never seen before. It always has to do with someone else. You may say, "Someone has got to do something about this." Be prepared for the Holy Spirit to say, "How about you?" John the Baptist was moved by the religious society that he faced. He began to cry out against it and became a voice in the wilderness. God often places us here, so we can be the voice leading others out of the wilderness.

There was over 400 years between the writings of Malachi in the Old Testament and Matthew in the New Testament. At the end of these 400 years, John the Baptist emerged. The current conditions of his nation, Israel, moved him to prophesy against the religious system of his day.

He saw a people who were caught up in a religious routine, but had no power in their relationship with God. God used him to speak out against the system and to prepare the way for Jesus to come into the earth. God used his voice to give birth to His plan in the earth. John was not in the wilderness just making a lot of noise. He had a consuming passion in him that was fueled by the Holy Spirit. He recognized his destiny in God and was moved by the Holy Spirit to speak the truth, even though it would cost him his life.

The voice of one crying in the wilderness: "Prepare the way of the Lord; make straight in the desert a highway for our God. Every valley shall be exalted and every mountain and hill brought low; the crooked places shall be made straight and the rough places smooth; the glory of the Lord shall be revealed, and all flesh shall see it together; for the mouth of the Lord has spoken" (Isaiah 40:3-5).

God is looking for a voice. He must have a voice in order to move in the earth the way He desires.

I was in Frankfurt, Germany preparing for a service one night and the Holy Spirit ministered to me out of Isaiah 40. He spoke to me like this: "The voice of one that crieth in Frankfurt, Germany—prepare ye the way of the Lord; make straight in Frankfurt a highway for our God. Every valley in Frankfurt will be exalted and every mountain and hill in Frankfurt will be brought low. The crooked places in Frankfurt will be made straight and the rough places will be made smooth; and the glory of the Lord shall be revealed in Frankfurt, Germany and all of Frankfurt shall see it together for the mouth of the Lord hath spoken it."

Now take the name of your church and city, and put it in the place of "Frankfurt" and begin to pray. It is a voice of intercession that God is looking for. God desires to pour out His Spirit, but there has to be a voice building a highway for Him.

Intercession is like building a highway. It will take time to see it completed. Our voice of intercession takes down the mountains and builds up the valleys. God is waiting for us. All He needs is someone to say, "I will be the voice to call upon Him for my land."

What every pastor is looking for are those who will join him in calling on the Lord for an awakening in his church.

The earnest heartfelt continued prayer of a righteous man makes tremendous power available dynamic in its working (James 5:16 AMP).

THE VOICE OF ONE MUST BECOME ONE VOICE

When the Lord said to me, "The voice of one," I prayed for several hours. After a time I heard the Holy Spirit say, "The voice of one must become one voice."

When the day of Pentecost had fully come, they were all with one accord in one place (Acts 2:1).

Their voices were in one accord (unity in heart, mind, and spirit), and they became the "voice of one." When this happened, the power of God fell on them and the New Testament church was born.

And suddenly there came a sound from heaven, as of a rushing mighty wind, and it filled the whole house where they were sitting. Then there appeared to them divided tongues, as of fire, and one sat upon each of them. And they were all filled with the Holy Spirit and began to speak with other tongues, as the Spirit gave them utterance (Acts 2:2-4).

Later in the Book of Acts, the disciples were under heavy persecution and began to seek the Lord.

"Now, Lord, look on their threats, and grant to Your servants that with all boldness they may speak Your word, by stretching out Your hand to heal, and that signs and wonders may be done through the name of Your holy Servant Jesus." And when they had prayed, the place where they were assembled together was shaken; and they were all filled with the Holy Spirit, and they spoke the word of God with boldness. Now the multitude of those who believed were of one heart and one soul; neither did anyone say that any of the things he possessed was his own, but they had all things in common (Acts 4:29-32).

The voice of one had become one voice. The power of God shook the place where they were assembled.

Ten years after the initial infilling of the Holy Spirit on the Day of Pentecost, God began to do something new. He was ready to pour out His Holy Spirit on the Gentiles. He had been looking for a Gentile man who was ready to receive.

*There was a **certain man** in Caesarea called Cornelius, a centurion of what was called the Italian Regiment, a devout man and one who feared God with all his household, who gave alms generously to the people, and prayed to God always* (Acts 10:1-2, emphasis added).

God always brings a new move of His Spirit in the earth through men and women of prayer.

God gave the apostle Peter a vision to prepare him for what He was about to do. God was getting ready to rock the Jews' religious minds (read Acts 10).

Peter witnessed the Holy Spirit being poured out on the Gentiles. He then knew God was no respector of persons. These Gentiles were serving the Lord, yet were not keepers of the law nor were they circumcised. Naturally we would think that everyone would be excited about this new move of the Spirit of God. However, contention quickly arose.

> *Now the apostles and brethren who were in Judea heard that the Gentiles had also received the word of God. And when Peter came up to Jerusalem, those of the circumcision* **contended** *with him* (Acts 11:1-2, emphasis added).

People rose up against the new move of God because it was something different than what they were used to. They also did not like the fact that the people were not Jewish, law keepers or circumcised. Immediately they tried to bring the people into bondage. As a result, strife came into the church.

> *Now about that time Herod the king stretched out his hand to harass some from the church. Then he killed James the brother of John with the sword* (Acts 12:1-2).

The church was so busy arguing over the new move of God, they allowed contention to replace prayer. Instead of fighting for the Kingdom of God, they were fighting against uncircumcised Gentiles entering the Kingdom.

As they fought among themselves, satan arose in Herod and he grabbed his opportunity to behead James. I do not believe it was the will of God for James to die at that time. It happened because strife and contention had filled the church and they had gotten away from prayer. It is very possible that if the church had been in the place of prayer, rather than strife, the life of James would have been saved.

Herod was planning to kill Peter the following day, so the church called an all-night prayer meeting. I am sure they were not discussing the problems of Gentile conversion that night. I am sure they no longer cared who was circumcised and who was not. They were joined in prayer for Peter to be delivered. And God sent an angel to deliver him.

Take a look at your church. Are you complaining over the color of the carpet? Are you upset with the pastor for teaching too much about tithing? Are you angry at what someone said about you, especially since you have been attending this church longer than they have? These things all lead to contention.

With the spirit of contention in place, it is no wonder the Church is not experiencing the power of God. It is no wonder people in our congregations are sick and dying. It is no wonder people are living defeated lives.

It is time for us to judge our hearts and get back to prayer and good works. When we do, we will see a hurting world turn to the Church for answers.

We have to take responsibility for ourselves. We need the spirit of Epaphras.

Epaphras, who is one of you, a bondservant of Christ, greets you, always laboring fervently for you in prayers, that you may stand perfect and complete in all the will of God (Colossians 4:12).

He labored fervently in prayer for the church at Colosse. Are you an Epaphras or a complainer? *Are you laboring in prayer for your pastor and your church, or are you spending most of your time speaking your mind and expressing your opinion on how things ought to be?* It is much easier to be a *critic* rather than to be a *contributor.* You can contribute greatly to the success of others through your prayers. We have labored hard, "wagging our tongues" about the things we don't like in our leaders; but have we labored hard "exercising our tongues" in passionate prayer on their behalf?

When a congregation gets away from what is eternal, like prayer, and steps into contention, the door is opened for satan to enter.

For where envy and self-seeking exist, confusion and every evil thing are there (James 3:16).

In this hour the Holy Spirit is drawing us together to become ONE VOICE. If we do not become one voice, God will look for the VOICE OF ONE.

God will find someone to cry out for revival. Let it be you. Make a difference for God in your local church. Tell your pastor that you are going to seek God for an outpouring of the Holy Spirit on his congregation.

Let's determine in our hearts to do what it takes to hear the Lord say, "Well done, good and faithful servant."

Chapter 5

It's Time to...

Stand With Your Pastor

The Tillerman
The husbandman of all the earth,
The skies, the lands, the seas,
Spoke to the North, South, East, and West
With bold authority.

"My only Son whom I have loved
Has bought a gift for Me."
As He unwrapped this precious prize,
I looked so I could see
A tiny plot of land that's worth
The greatest price He paid on Earth.

"There inside My dear Son's hand
I looked upon this piece of land.
A barren field, an empty place
It's full of stumps and weeds and waste."

"I will need a volunteer to come
And work this land of Mine.
A Tillerman to dig and plant
And water when it's time."

Silence fell across the lands,
The skies and all the seas.

99

No hand was raised, no voice was heard,
Just silence from His plea.

But from across the world there came
A voice still young but strong.
"I'll till the soil, I'll work this lot
As if it were my own."

He dug his hands into the soil,
Day and night he toiled and toiled.
With faith and love and hope as seeds,
He spent his life to plant these trees.
A bud, a blade, a stem, a tree,
The field was growing so beautifully.

A tree still stands upon this place
A tree whose roots are true.
You see, the empty field was me
And my Tillerman was you.

⊙⊙⊙⊙⊙⊙⊙⊙⊙

My wife, Kim Nance, wrote this poem for a mentor who had invested both time and love in her life, helping her become what she is today. Every believer has someone who is a tillerman in his or her life—someone who has influenced their lives for God.

If we stop and think about our pastor and his place in our lives, we will most likely discover that he is a tillerman. The majority of us were the field that needed much work. God set a pastor over us, bringing us to the place we are today.

Most of us have never taken the time to say, "thank you" to these men and women who have toiled to make our lives fruitful. No pastor is perfect, but irregardless we need to give him honor for the patience he has demonstrated while helping us.

A great evangelist was once asked why he didn't run for the presidency of the United States. He simply replied, "Why step down?"

I like that answer. God calls and appoints pastors and spiritual leaders—men do not. They are not elected by a church board to walk in the office of pastor. The call comes from Heaven.

A tillerman is someone who holds the position of a spiritual father in our lives. He or she is set in our lives as an example, to help bring us to the place where God wants us to be. We must always remember that just as we haven't chosen our families or earthly fathers, neither do we choose our spiritual fathers; God does. They are in our lives by God's choice to polish, prune and perfect us. Never underestimate the power of the influence that the man of God will have upon your life.

These men and women who have spoken into our lives should be held up in high esteem and honor. When you honor the men and women God has sent to you, you also honor the One who has sent them.

I watched one Sunday morning as my pastor and his wife fought with their umbrellas trying to get out of the car into the church without getting soaked during a rainstorm. At that moment I said to myself, "That will be the last time that will happen." I went to work and developed a group of men and women assigned to the pastors to aid them in and out of church. If it was a hot day, we made sure their car was cool. If it was cold outside, we made sure their car was warm. Never again did they have to be concerned about getting wet. I did not organize this ministry to earn any points with them; I simply did it out of honor. Neither did they demand that I do this. It was just a small service we could perform to give honor to the office they held.

God has blessed me in so many great ways, and many of these blessings have been poured upon me because of works just like this one. My wife and I have determined to bless the Tillermen in our lives and God has, in return, blessed us. When you give a prophet a cup of water in the name of a prophet, you will receive a prophet's reward.

There are several important aspects to standing with and supporting our pastors.

WE ARE TO STAND WITH THEM, NOT BEHIND THEM

Several years ago I was visiting with another minister and he asked me, "How does it feel to stand in your pastor's shadow?"

Before I even had time to think of a reply I spoke, "I don't know how it feels because I have never stood behind him; I have always stood *with* him."

I know that came out of my spirit because it was so simple and so true. We are never in anyone's shadow if we are standing beside them. We are only in someone's shadow if we are standing behind them. Many church members are behind their pastor instead of beside him because they are not assisting in bringing the vision to pass.

In 1983, the Lord spoke to me about becoming an armorbearer to my pastor. When He spoke this, He told to me to "run with the vision of the house." I will never forget that. When God raises up a church, He speaks to the pastor and gives him a vision for that local church body. That vision is what I call the "vision of the house."

This "vision of the house" is not just the personal vision of the pastor, but the direction God is leading that particular church through the leadership of the pastor. It is up to every individual of that local body of believers to ask God where they fit into the vision. If we will make up our minds to run with that vision, we will find ourselves coming into the call that God has placed on our lives. *What we make happen for someone else, God will make happen for us.*

"Now, Lord, look on their threats, and grant to Your servants that with all boldness they may speak Your word, by stretching out Your hand to heal,

and that signs and wonders may be done through the name of Your holy Servant Jesus." And when they had prayed, the place where they were assembled together was shaken; and they were all filled with the Holy Spirit, and they spoke the word of God with boldness (Acts 4:29-31).

Now I call that revival! The actual building where they were praying was shaken. This could happen today. The key to the manifestation of this power is found in verse 32, "Now the multitude that believed was of one heart and one soul."

There is a difference between *one heart* and *one soul*. *One heart* means we are connected because we are members of the Body of Christ. *One soul* means we are running together with the same vision. That vision is the "vision of the house," the one God has given to our pastor for our local church body.

If everyone in the local church today would start uniting heart and soul with their pastor, could you imagine what would take place? I can tell you. We would take the world for God.

Many of you reading this right now know in your heart that you have not been standing with your pastor. Well, now is the time. Go to your pastor, realize his vision and begin to run with it. Then watch what will happen in your life.

Always remember, what you make happen for someone else God makes happen for you.

THE ANOINTING STARTS AT THE HEAD

Psalm 133:1-2 says, "Behold how good and how pleasant it is for brethren to dwell together in unity! It is like the precious oil upon the head, running down on the beard, the beard of Aaron. Running down on the edge of his garments."

When Aaron was anointed, oil was poured on his head and flowed down to the rest of his body. This Scripture links unity with the anointing.

If there is going to be unity in a local church, the members must understand that the anointing begins at the head and flows to the rest of the body. The head of the Body of Christ is Jesus the Great Shepherd and the undershepherds He has placed over the local church are the pastors. The Lord has called pastors and placed them as overseers of that body of believers. This means that if we are going to flow in the anointing, we need to be in a place where that flow of anointing can impact our lives.

The apostle Paul told Timothy to stir up the gifts that are within, through the laying on of his hands. I believe that it is scriptural to transfer anointing into another man's life by the laying on of hands of the men and women of God. Moses laid his hands on 80 elders so that they could deal with the people using the same spirit he had. Elisha received a double portion of the anointing on Elijah. God said that He will take of your spirit and put it on them.

I believe the pastor is the spiritual authority of the local church and that he carries an anointing; and by being around the pastor and spending time with him, a transfer of his anointing can take place.

God wants us serving (or functioning) under our pastor's anointing. If we want to operate in the place that God has for us, we must keep ourselves under the authority of our pastors, because God has set them over us. Once we are in that place, we must stay connected.

God breathes on what is connected. God formed Adam from the dirt of the earth, and once formed, He breathed into him the breath of life. Adam was connected before the breath of God came.

If we were to examine a severed human hand, it would most likely turn our stomachs. But if that severed hand began to move, we would say, "That's spooky. How can a hand that is cut off from the body move on its own?"

In the Church today, we are witnessing severed parts of the Body that seem to be moving on their own. All I can say about them is, they are spooky. They seem to move in and out of local churches with mysterious gifts and callings. They always appear to be super-spiritual, yet they have no accountability in their lives. The bottom line is they are not connected. We are living in the last days and Jesus warned us about this very thing. He identified them as wolves in sheep's clothing.

THE APOSTLES WERE ACCOUNTABLE TO ONE ANOTHER

And I went up by revelation, and communicated to them that gospel which I preach among the Gentiles, but privately to those who were of reputation, lest by any means I might run, or had run, in vain (Galatians 2:2).

The apostle Paul, who wrote two-thirds of the New Testament, went to the apostles at Jerusalem and submitted his teaching to them. He asked them to ensure his message was of God and that he was not running his race in vain.

Paul, being called of God, did not have to go to these men and have them approve what he was teaching. The Bible tells us in Second Corinthians 12:2 that Paul was "caught up to the third heaven." He received revelation directly from Jesus. Considering from where Paul received his revelation, it is understandable that submission to these men was not the easiest thing for him to do.

So why was it necessary for him to submit to men? Paul was led by the Holy Spirit to go to Jerusalem, because the Holy Spirit knew the importance of accountability and spiritual authority.

If the Body of Christ would learn from this, we would keep false doctrine out of the Church. Just because we get a revelation does not mean it is from God. We need to take it to our pastor and other leaders who are in authority over us and lay it before them, to help us determine if it is a Bible-based revelation before giving it out. This applies to leaders as well as laymen. We, as leaders, have the God-given responsibility to make sure what we are presenting to the Body of Christ is in line with Scripture.

I have scrutinized some of the teaching I have heard over the years from men and women who have no accountability in their lives. I have found that some of this teaching was not founded on the Word of God and could lead to deception and destruction. It sounded good, but their revelation could not be proven in the Scriptures. Yet, some people thought it was the hottest revelation in town. It was presented as though God had spoken and no one dared to question the revelation. The problem is, if you cannot find chapter and verse in the Bible, you had better not accept it as truth—and I don't care who teaches it.

I am disturbed by the lack of spiritual accountability in our independent churches and organizations. We need to take a look at the Bible and see what took place at the Council of Jerusalem in Acts 15:4-29. The ministers at this Council had to decide whether they should allow Gentile converts to come into fellowship with Jews, without following the law of Moses.

This decision was going to bring major change in the minds of the believers and set a precedent. The apostles went to the Scripture and then heard testimony from Paul and Barnabas. There was discussion and prayer before a decision was made.

...in the multitude of counselors there is safety (Proverbs 11:14).

This is exactly what I am referring to when I talk about accountability. I challenge those in positions of leadership to establish a group of men and women of integrity, who are not afraid to question each other or be questioned concerning the doctrines they preach and teach.

Several years ago someone submitted a teaching curriculum for my approval. They had personally written this curriculum and wanted to teach it in one of our Sunday morning Bible classes. When I looked at the curriculum, I noticed a statement I did not agree with, and I knew my pastor would not agree with it either.

I spoke to the author of the material and said that this particular statement would have to be reworded or left out entirely. Immediately the person responded, "Well, I would be afraid to touch it because God gave it to me."

I explained to the person that God had appointed me to oversee this department in the church, and it was my responsibility to make sure that no doctrinal conflicts occurred between the pulpit and other areas of the church. Then I took out an eraser and did my job.

Now I plead with you, brethren, by the name of our Lord Jesus Christ, that you all speak the same thing, and that there be no divisions among you, but that you be perfectly joined together in the same mind and in the same judgment (1 Corinthians 1:10).

This Scripture says we should all speak the same thing. In other words, we should all be of the same mind.

Now I realize in the worldwide Body of Christ we will not all agree on every doctrine; but in the local body of believers we all must speak the same thing. If someone teaches a Bible class contradicting the pastor and leadership, a door is opened for strife and division to enter the local church.

It is time we stay submitted to our leadership and determine to stay connected with the local church where God has placed us.

WE ARE TO BE A SUPPORT TO OUR PASTORS

The word *support* means, "that which supports or upholds, a sustainer, a comforter, a maintainer, a defender."

God is looking for people to uphold, comfort, maintain, and defend their pastor. He is looking for people who will stand with their pastor even in seasons of trials and difficulties. It is easy to stand with them when all is going well, but what happens when your leaders face a season of trouble? If you have been faithful in a local church, you have probably already witnessed something that has tried to shake your pastor away from his calling.

Satan knows that if he can destroy the pastor, he can scatter the sheep. That's why God is looking for men and women who are committed to prayer and standing in the gap for their pastor, refusing to let the devil get any foothold in his life.

When you decide to be this kind of church member, God will use you to speak into your pastor's life in times of need. He will use you to be an encouragement. Your pastor will receive this ministry because he will have confidence in your support of him.

I remember a special teaching seminar that we were having in our church many years ago. As the meeting started on Saturday morning, the guest minister asked how many people were visiting from other churches. When the hands went up, we could not believe it. The auditorium was packed that day, but less than a third of our members had attended.

When I looked at my pastor's face, I could see disappointment all over him. I was frustrated as well; we had planned this seminar to be a blessing, especially for our church members—yet they did not come. It was great that the building was full, but it was mostly visitors who were there. Many people drove from different states, but our own people would not even drive across town to attend. There is nothing that hurts and disappoints a pastor more than having a special meeting and the members don't think enough of it to even show up.

The meeting ended Saturday night, and we then had regular services on Sunday. On Sunday morning, I noticed that my pastor was very quiet.

When it came time for the message, he had everyone working in the audio and television departments turn off their equipment and come sit with the congregation.

When everyone was in place, Pastor walked out into the congregation and began to share his heart with them. It was not a rebuke, but he wanted to be honest. He asked several people to share with him why they did not attend this seminar. Several reasons were given—some people were on vacation, some were busy with their children and families, and some said they just did not come.

Suddenly, a lady from the congregation came forward and shared a vision the Lord had shown her concerning the pastor. In her vision, Pastor anointed each person in the congregation with oil. As he did, each of us made a fresh, new commitment to him and to run with the vision of the house.

We knew this was from the Holy Spirit, so we formed a line on both sides of the church and began a prayer service. The presence of the Lord was in the house and it was evident that God was doing something extraordinary.

I was standing in the prayer line when the Holy Spirit began to speak to me. He said, "I want you to wash your pastor's feet." This conviction was so heavy on me that I knew I would become sick if I did not do it. I don't have a problem with washing someone's feet, but I had never done anything like that before.

I got out of the line and went to a room next to the stage. Standing in the hall, I told the Lord that I would obey, but I wanted to know why He chose me. The Holy Spirit said, "Terry, you are to do this as a representative of the congregation." He told me that since I had been there from the beginning, no one else could better represent this congregation.

I had no doubt that this was the Lord. As the anointing service was concluding, I came out on the stage and asked Pastor to come up to the stage with me. I told both Pastor and the congregation what the Lord had instructed me to do. As I began washing my pastor's feet, everyone, including Pastor and myself, began to weep. Several in the congregation fell to their faces sobbing.

When I had finished, I stood for over 20 minutes while my pastor sat in a chair, crying before the Lord. It was one of the most powerful moves of the Holy Spirit that I have ever witnessed. I realized that foot washing ministered more to the one receiving it than the one giving it. God truly did something marvelous that day in our church and ministered to my pastor in a way that only He can.

When God needs someone to speak a word of encouragement, He will use only those who are true supporters of their pastor. I pray that you will let God use you in lifting up your pastor.

WE MUST LEARN TO HONOR OUR PASTOR AND LEADERS

The word *honor* means, "the esteem due or paid to something of worth." It is a testimony or an expression of respect expressed through words or actions.

Honor and respect are different. Respect is an attitude. Honor is an action. To honor someone is to take respect to a higher level. We can have respect for someone but never honor him. When we take the step to do something for them, we are giving them honor.

Honor is something we give to God and to people. The Bible tells us to give honor and praise to God; it also tells us to honor one another. Honor is something we give.

We honor our pastors by being on time for church services. We honor them by making sure we are there for special meetings. We honor them by getting involved in the ministry of helps. We honor our pastor by giving our tithes to the church. We honor them by making sure that they and their families are well taken care of. We honor them by making ourselves available to them for anything they may need. We honor them when we rise to the place of our calling; we honor them when we are faithful in our business; and we honor them when we become effective witnesses in our community. And while these things honor our pastor, they also honor God.

Let the elders who rule well be counted worthy of double honor, especially those who labor in the word and doctrine (1 Timothy 5:17).

The word *honor* here means "to value or to esteem to the highest degree."

How would we honor the state governor if he or she were coming to visit our church? We would go out of our way to make sure everything was set up and ready. We would assign our very best people to meet their every need. Why would we do this? It would be out of honor for the office they hold. We may not necessarily agree with their position on certain issues, but we would give honor to them for their office.

The Bible declares we are not just to give honor to spiritual leaders, but also to give them *double* honor. The word *double* in Strong's Concordance means "two-fold." In other words, we should be doing *twice* as much for our pastors and spiritual leaders than what we do for our political leaders.

It appears to me that the Church has some catching up to do. We have fallen far behind in honoring our leaders.

Stop and think about the last time you told your pastor that you love and appreciate all he does. I challenge you to take time today and be a blessing in his life in some way. Then watch what will happen in your life when you do this.

NEVER SPEAK AGAINST YOUR PASTOR

I had been working at our church for just a few short years when a situation arose that taught me a very valuable lesson.

I was asked to assist with the tape ministry when the department fell behind on making tapes. I was working with a young man who was in charge of the tape ministry. As we worked, he complained about his job. He did not like the way things operated in the ministry, and he began to speak against several people in leadership and to criticize the pastor.

As a coworker I could understand how he felt in some areas, but I also knew he was offended and that the offense had taken hold of him, spurring his discontent. I listened for a while—but then I knew enough had been said.

I told him that I knew he was offended and that he had to get rid of it or it would destroy his ministry. He had the call of God on his life, but all he was displaying was a rebellious attitude. I encouraged him to sit down with Pastor and talk it out, so he could get rid of the bitterness and resentment.

I had worked at the church for years and had always appreciated Pastor's integrity. I knew him to be a man who would listen to what you had to say and give you a fair answer as he saw it. Although I encouraged this man to stop talking to me and go directly to the pastor, it had no effect on him. It was not what he wanted to hear. His real desire was not change or reconciliation, but for me to join his cause. I refused.

When I finished with the tapes and returned to my office, the phone rang. It was Pastor asking me to come and see him.

I immediately went to his office and he asked me to have a seat. He began by telling me how much he appreciated me. I was blessed to hear it, but it was the first time I was called to his office just to be told something like this.

Then he told me why he wanted me to know of his regard. He had gone into the break room to get something to drink (the break room was right next to the tape duplication room), and he had overheard the entire conversation I had just had with the other employee. He told me how blessed he was to hear my response and that he appreciated me for it.

I must be very honest—when he was talking, I think my heart skipped a few beats. Just the very thought of talking about my pastor and having him overhear that conversation was horrifying.

I thanked Pastor and returned to my office with shaky legs. When I got to my office I shut the door, looked up to Heaven and said, "Thank You, Jesus! Thank You, Jesus! I kept my mouth shut!"

The truth is, I have had opportunities to be offended, but I have refused to allow the offense to stay with me.

As I look back on this incident after nearly 20 years have passed, I realize that had I joined in on that conversation and criticized the pastor, my ministry today would probably not be what God intended for it to be. This one event, speaking against my pastor, could have set my call off course. I would have hurt Pastor and his trust in me would have been broken. It may have taken years for that trust to be regained, if ever.

One morning during his Sunday message, Pastor, out of the clear blue, began to tell of that incident in the tape room. He has never forgotten it. As he told the story, just like all those years ago, my knees started feeling a little weak. Again I said under my breath, "Thank You, Jesus, I kept my mouth shut." Once again the image came to me of what could have happened had I joined in and began to criticize.

The truth behind this is, that even if no one can overhear your conversation, God is still listening. Judging another person will only hurt you. Why? Because you are actually guilty of the very thing with which you are condemning them.

Therefore you are inexcusable, O man, whoever you are who judge, for in whatever you judge another you condemn yourself; for you who judge practice the same things (Romans 2:1).

REALIZE THAT OUR PASTORS ARE HUMAN

I have often said that it is harder to work with a Christian staff than it is to work with non-Christian employees. We expect Christians to conduct themselves like Christ. When they act like someone who is not saved, we are shocked. We expect them to be perfect because they are born again.

A man approached me at church one day and told me that the Lord had spoken to him to keep the lawn at my home mowed all summer. I quickly responded, "I know that's God." As far as I am concerned, yard work is under the curse. I was delighted that God would bless me in this way.

The first Saturday he came out early in the morning and began work-ing. Saturday was my only day off, and I enjoy playing tennis and golf. As I walked out with my tennis racquet, I thanked him for his blessing before heading out to play tennis. When I returned, he was finished, and I was very pleased with the work he had done. The next Saturday was the same. I came out in the morning, and he was working in my yard. Again, I told him how much I appreciated his work and left to play tennis.

When the third Saturday rolled around and he did not show up, I wondered what had happened to him. He never returned.

After a few weeks, it dawned on me that in some way I had offended him. When we finally met in church one Sunday, I asked him if there was a problem or if I had offended him in some way. He said, "Yes, you have."

I apologized and asked him what I had done. He said, "You went and played tennis while I was mowing your yard. As a minister, you should have been using that time to pray and read the Bible."

A lightbulb lit up inside me; the problem was just revealed. He had a religious spirit and was trying to condemn me. I told him that he needed to realize I was human like everyone else. Saturday was my only day off and I found relaxation in playing tennis. I told him even God took a day off; and when God rested, He didn't do yard work.

Many laypeople want to put their leaders on a pedestal that they can-not stay on. No one is perfect but Jesus. I am not making excuses for sin, carnality or living according to the flesh. We, as spiritual leaders, are called to a higher standard; but laypeople need to realize that pastors must have some time to relax and be themselves.

I often teach on intercessory prayer and lead prayer meetings in the church. After teaching on intimacy with God one night, a lady came to me and said, "Oh, Brother Terry, if I could just be a fly and fly around your house all day long and hear you worship God, it would just be the most wonderful thing!"

I laughed to myself. I thought if there was a fly flitting around my house, it wouldn't be long before it was squashed under a flyswatter.

In some people's minds, spiritual leaders should spend all their time in prayer and worship. However, we all have to deal with the common issues of life. I have three children at home plus many church responsibilities. Just like everyone else, I have to make time to pray and spend with the Lord.

Our leaders are human. We must realize that and give them room to be themselves and even make mistakes. The greatest respect we can have for a man or woman of God is to recognize the human side of their lives, while at the same time respecting the office of authority in which they stand.

The World of Dr. Smith and Brother Jones

The first ten years I worked for Agape Church, I was responsible for the transportation and comfort of all the guest speakers whom we had ministering at our annual camp meeting. Over the years as I did this, I discovered these ministers each had a different personality, different habits, different likes and dislikes. While most were very kind and easy to work with, a few were quite challenging.

Since it is not my intention to embarrass anyone, but to merely illustrate a point, I will change the names of the ministers I am using for my example. I will call them Brother Jones and Dr. Smith.

Dr. Smith was a great apostle and a very powerful man of God. When he came to minister at the church, I would always have a vehicle and driver at his disposal. This allowed him to go anywhere at anytime, making everything as easy as possible for him. He was a man who liked everything a certain way and was very direct in his communication, to the point of being offensive at times.

Brother Jones was quite another character. I never knew what he would do, when he would show up or if he would spontaneously change his schedule without telling anyone. These two men were total opposites.

Since I had not received any communication from Brother Jones regarding his itinerary, on the day he was to speak I was *still* trying to find out when he would be arriving. No one, including his secretary, knew where he was or when he would arrive. I was totally dependent upon him just to show up and be on time.

Sure enough, just a few hours before the meeting started, he called my pastor and told him his plane would be landing in a few minutes. Pastor went to the airport, picked him up and took him to the hotel. (In the meantime, Pastor called me to let me know what was happening so I could stop trying to locate our guest.)

The service was to begin at 7:00 p.m., so I sent a driver to pick him up at his hotel at 6:45 p.m. I waited at the church to receive him and make him comfortable. However, when the driver arrived at the hotel he found that Brother Jones had checked out. No one at the hotel knew where he had gone and I had no idea where he could be.

I later discovered Brother Jones liked to swim. Since it was early May, most of the swimming pools in town were still closed for the season, including the hotel we put him in. However, he had called around town until he had found a small hotel that would allow him to swim in their pool. Even though he was happy with the new swimming arrangements, we had no idea where he was.

At 7:00 p.m. Pastor looked at me and asked, "Where is Brother Jones?" All I could do was tell him the truth—"He checked out."

The service began on time. Forty minutes later, Brother Jones finally arrived to explain the hotel and the swimming situation. Needless to say, I was not a happy camper. The only problem was, things got worse.

Brother Jones preached the first night of our weeklong camp meeting and then stayed to hear Dr. Smith minister in a pastors' meeting the following afternoon. Since Dr. Smith was very punctual and precise, I spent time going over his schedule with him so he would have a full understanding of how everything would flow. He told me he would minister for 55 minutes, then turn the service over to Pastor. Pastor was to dismiss the meeting while I quickly escorted Dr. Smith and his wife out the door to the waiting car and right to the airport. Since Dr. Smith was a regular guest minister here, it was standard procedure. No problem; we did this for him all the time.

All seemed to be going according to plan, a relief after the confusion of the previous night. However, what I did not know was that during the meeting, Brother Jones had slipped in and had slipped out again five minutes before Dr. Smith had concluded. Brother Jones then got into Dr. Smith's waiting car and asked to be taken to his hotel.

When I walked Dr. and Mrs. Smith to their waiting car, it was not waiting. There was no car and there was no driver.

I was in total shock. This could not be happening to me. I can still remember Dr. Smith staring straight ahead and, in his deep voice, demanding, "Where is my car?"

I looked around for anyone who might know what happened to the car and driver. An usher came over to explain that Brother Jones had taken the car to his hotel and the driver would return for the Smiths in about ten minutes.

My heart dropped. I felt as low as a person can feel. I thought, *Oh no, my name just got blotted out of the Lamb's Book of Life.* I had offended the present-day apostle Paul; I had lost his donkey.

I profusely apologized and asked if I could get another car and personally drive them to the airport. Dr. Smith just kept looking straight ahead and said, "No."

So, I asked if I could escort them to the pastor's office and get them something to drink while we waited for the driver to return. He said, "No."

I asked if I could at least take him to our minister's guest room. He said, "No." He told me he would only leave in that particular car and with that particular driver. So, I just had to leave him standing there.

As you can imagine, I was not having a good time at camp meeting. When I went back into the church, Pastor met me inside the door and asked, "Terry, what is Dr. Smith doing standing outside?" I explained what had happened and Pastor told me to get his own car and take the Smiths to the airport. Again, I explained that I had already offered and Dr. Smith refused to do anything but stand outside and wait for his car and driver.

I was frustrated and aggravated. To make it worse, as I walked toward the auditorium a door greeter said to me, "Smile, Brother Terry."

I know I must have given her a look that could maim, if not kill. For just a moment I thought, *I'm not going to smile and you can't make me smile.*

I relate this story to give you an example of the human side of ministry. We all face days like this. Super-spiritual people try to blame these days on the devil. However, it was not the devil that caused the entire situation; it was Brother Jones in his impulsiveness and Dr. Smith in his unbending determination to have everything just so. The devil did not have a thing to do with it.

I am sure the devil looks at God sometimes and says, "Now wait a minute, I didn't have a thing to do with that one."

We live in a world of people and personalities. With those personalities come simple problems because no one is perfect. We need to cut pastors, ministers and the church staff some slack. They are doing the best they can, walking in love while serving the Body of Christ. They are not perfect and at times will offend and will make plenty of mistakes. But it is time to stand with the leaders and work together to accomplish the job.

Even though these two men were a little moody, to say the least, God honored me. I refused to get offended and made a mental note to not act that way as a leader. You will win if you determine that you will not allow yourself to be hurt when you see the human side of leaders.

A STAFF OF USED CARS

I heard the pastor of a very large ministry once say his staff was like a fleet of used cars—they always needed something.

After hearing that, I went home and the thought of being a used car kept running through my mind. I had served at that time in the same local church for over 22 years; and if I am like a used car, then I have a lot of mileage on me. I began to pray and ask the Lord to help me be a good used car. After praying, I was given a revelation from the Lord about church staff that I believe will help you.

How are staff members like used cars?

1. *A used car is better than a new car if the new car is never driven.* If a car sits idle and is never taken out of the driveway, it never benefits anyone. Far too many church members do nothing, like new cars that never leave the driveway. At least the church staff and the ministry of helps have made the decision to do something. Praise God for that. When working with people, there will be problems, but it is better to deal with the problems than, as a pastor, to have to do everything yourself.

2. *Whether we purchase a used car or a new one, after a week they both begin to depreciate.* The problem in many ministries is that after a week, the new staff members become "de-appreciated."

As leaders, if we are not careful, it is easy to take for granted one of our most valuable assets—our staff. We often take our car for granted and as long as it works, we don't give it much attention. However, at some point maintenance will be required to keep it in good running order. *We must be careful not to use people to build the vision. People are the vision.* The saying is true, "People don't care how much you know until they know how much you care."

3. *All cars must be maintained.* Every 3,000 to 5,000 miles the old oil must be flushed out and replaced with fresh. As leaders it is not enough to just expect our staff to be in church—we need to invest time praying with them for the vision of the house and their own personal needs. It

is through prayer and prayer alone that the vision will be kept alive in our staff.

Every 30,000 miles a car requires a tune-up. Just like our car, our staff needs a good tune-up about once a year. Once a year our ministerial staff would take a few days to relax and pray. It was something I always looked forward to. It gave me a new fire to press on. Even Jesus pulled the disciples aside to rest. Let's remember we still live in natural bodies that require rest and relaxation. So we must take some time, along with our staff, to rest and enjoy life and the ministry.

4. *A car we have owned for years that has never given us any major problems is faithful and worth keeping.* As leaders, we must hang on to those who have been faithful to us and let them set the example before the church. If there is a constant turnover in church staff, there is a problem somewhere. I know of a church where the nameplate for the youth director is actually a small chalkboard because the turnover is so great and because they grew tired of ordering new nameplates. All they have to do is erase the name of the former director and write in the new one. Now that is pitiful.

5. *A used car can either be low maintenance or high maintenance.* Staff members are either high or low maintenance, as well. If you are on a church staff, there is a way to tell if you are high or low maintenance. Just ask yourself this question: When my pastor sees me coming, does he smile or does he run for cover? No matter our position in the church, staff member or church member, we should all determine in our hearts to be low maintenance people who are a blessing to everyone around.

6. *No matter how much we like a car or how much we have paid for it, if it continually causes us problems, we have a lemon.* There is no choice; we have to get rid of it. How can we tell if we have a lemon? That person has a sour attitude. I heard John Maxwell say, "Why pay someone who is on your staff to be negative? There are plenty of people who are negative and you don't have to pay them a dime." A true shepherd knows how to separate out those who are "troubled" people from those who are there only to cause

trouble. With the troubled people the pastor will be patient and loving in his counseling and training. However, those who are there only to cause trouble and dissension must be weeded out so that they do not adversely affect the life of other members of the Body.

The level on which an airplane flies in relation to the horizon is called attitude. When a pilot is flying into a head wind, it is important to keep the attitude of the plane level in order to press through and not lose time and fuel. He will put the full thrust on the engines and fly through the head wind. If the pilot pulls the nose of the plane up, the plane will begin to slow. It will continue to fly, but it will be much more difficult because the attitude is not level. If he pulls the nose up even further, the plane will eventually stall. If the plane stalls, it will fall out of the sky even with the throttle at full speed.

Many staff members, along with the average church attendee, GET THEIR NOSES UP! We say, "Well bless God, the pastor preached too long today and his message offended me. Bless God, I'm not going to give the church my entire tithe. Bless God, I don't like the way his wife treats the people."

Each time we are offended and keep the offense in our heart, our life begins to stall. We may still feel God in our lives; we may still have the thrust, but our life is falling apart and we are in a stall because WE TURNED OUR NOSES UP! We are in pride and sin because of our attitude. It's time to adjust our attitude and let God get us back on track.

7. *If we keep our car long enough, eventually it will be deemed an antique and the value will be greater now than when we bought it.* Sometimes a car is not appreciated when it first goes into production, yet after years of faithful service, it is considered a valuable antique. An antique is considered a classic. The definition of a *classic* is being "an excellent model of its kind, balanced, formal and simple." If staff members determine to be a blessing and allow God to work in their lives, they will be considered a classic and their stature in the sight of the people will change. They will be viewed as an

excellent model, balanced and a good example of character and fortitude. They may not have all the ability they would like, but if they have longevity, they will be a great blessing to their pastor and their local church.

Let's set a goal to be a blessing to our pastors so we will be of value to them and the Lord.

Chapter 6

It's Time to...
Become Kingdom-Minded Leaders

It has been said that everything in the ministry will rise and fall based on leadership. That statement carries a lot of truth and especially in the local church. I feel everyone reading this book has leadership potential in them. We all are called by God to lead in some way, whether it is in business, church or at home. God is truly calling each of us to a higher calling, which will always lead to a new level of leadership in our lives.

In the last few years God has raised up many men to challenge Christian leaders to new levels of leadership. I believe these men teach the leader how to relate to the people. I know God has also given me an assignment to teach people how to relate to the leader.

In the last chapter I talked about standing with your pastor. I believe God has given me an assignment to teach men and women how to be an Aaron and Hur to their leader. Aaron and Hur were people who held up the arms of their leader through the good times and the bad. But in order for there to be real victory in the battle, there must also be men of God like Moses who will give themselves for a people, and not just for a vision.

As important as it is for each of us to understand our role in the Body of Christ and begin to step into our place, it is just as important that those called to walk in the office of an apostle, prophet, evangelist, teacher or pastor continue to grow and develop in their leadership skills.

These men and women hold an office that is not elected by men, but by God. You don't just wake up one day and decide that you want to go into full-time ministry. This is a calling from God, but with it comes great responsibility. These men and women will be held accountable before

God according to how they ministered and cared for the sheep to whom God assigned them.

In studying one day about God rejecting King Saul and choosing David, I discovered some powerful truths. It's hard to believe that a God who is so merciful would ever declare such a word as First Samuel 16:1, "I have rejected him." How far do we have to go to finally realize that God could be rejecting us. I know this sounds hard to believe but James 4:6 says, "God resists the proud." That word *resist* means that God rejects or sets Himself against. It is possible to get so lifted up in pride that we have moved into a place that God Himself is resisting us. When you reach that place, all the binding of the enemy will not help because the devil is not the problem; it is your own pride. True repentance is the only answer for your life.

Saul was not a *kingdom builder* but an *empire builder*. He was out for himself and fought to see that his empire remained in his control. He was very abusive and used people for his own advantage. He ended up losing everything because he thought only of himself. He was a leader who was known for his spiritual abuse.

My heart grieves when I have counseled people who have been through spiritual abuse. They are hurt, beat up and bleeding sheep. They want to run from the church and never come back. In the natural I don't blame them; but the truth of it is, that is not the answer. They need to seek God, find a pastor who will love and reach out to them and stay connected in a good local church.

I have been very blessed to have leaders who have allowed me to run with the call on my life—leaders who did not stop me, but encouraged me from a young age until now. I started working on a church staff when I was 17 years old. My first staff position was as a youth director in a small Assembly of God church. That pastor invested much in me to help in my teaching and preaching. I would walk into church 15 minutes before the service on many a Sunday night and he would say to me, "Terry, did I forget to tell you that tonight you were preaching?" The first few times I thought I would pass out, but He always encouraged me, saying that if I was called, the anointing would be there. He did that because he loved and believed in me. He taught me to never go to church without a sermon in my heart. This man was one of the greatest encouragers I had ever met. He constantly told me, "Terry, God has big plans for you, and you will do great things for Him."

I was fortunate to have the support of my pastor when I was ready to write my first book. He encouraged me and raised the money to have it printed. Without the support of these men I would not be where I am today. These are the kind of leaders God is looking for today to invest in the next generation. Unfortunately, not everyone has had these types of leaders to speak into their lives.

Many of you reading this book may relate more to the bruised and the hurt, than you can to the love and understanding. If you are one who has been abused, please do not lose trust in leadership.

On a positive note, you must understand that for every *one* Christian leader who is bad, there are *hundreds* who love God and are doing their best for God's people.

I want to take this chapter and turn the coin around to look at the other side of leadership. I believe we need to stand with our leaders and be faithful to them through the thick of the battle. But I also know that the pastor must be willing to lay down his life for the sheep. Jesus said the good shepherd will give his life for his sheep.

Let's take a look at the leadership of Saul and where he missed it. We will look at the difference between empire builders and kingdom builders.

CHARACTERISTICS OF AN EMPIRE BUILDER

He will take.

In First Samuel 8 God tells Samuel that the leader the people want "will take…will take…will take…and he will take." In other words, "He will be on the take." Saul was only in it for himself. It was all about, "What is in it for me?" What about my feelings; how does this decision affect me; and what will happen to my ministry? It is always about what will benefit me.

These leaders are not kingdom builders; they are empire builders. They have a goal of building an empire that displays their greatness and their talents. To work for them, you will have to sign something, requiring that everything you create be given to them or the ministry. Doing this actually stops the creativity from flowing, but they feel they must carefully guard the empire. Many times these leaders are sincere at the beginning and are truly trying to do all things for God, but they become so vision driven that whoever can't keep up is discarded as having no faith.

Saul guarded his empire and protected it at all cost. He eyed everyone around him and especially those close to him. He actually thought the kingdom belonged to him.

Empire builders will manipulate, dominate and intimidate.

Saul was possessed with the need to control everything and everyone around him. He wanted and had absolute power. The saying is true that *absolute power corrupts absolutely.*

Have you ever witnessed a sheep that is nervous, scared and worried about what the shepherd was going to do to them that day? A sheep knows the care the shepherd has for them and knows that the shepherd has his best interest in mind.

When people are scared to come into the presence of a Christian leader, something is wrong. I totally understand respect, but if people are hesitant to share how they feel because they fear some kind of retribution, then something in the atmosphere of the ministry is wrong. That leader has become untouchable.

Saul used control and intimidation to keep all his servants in check. The servants lived in fear due to his mood swings. They were calling for David to come so that he could play and sing to lessen Saul's distress. They did not know from one day to the next which personality they would have to contend with. This style of leadership leads to a paranoid mind. The leader feels everyone is out to take advantage of him, and He loses touch with reality itself. He trusts no one.

They are positional leaders.

Saul led from his authority "top down." He used that position to make his decisions knowing that no one could question him.

It is very important in the day we live in, to have people who can speak objectively into our lives. These are people who are not just on the payroll; these are people who hold you accountable for your actions the way you hold your staff accountable for theirs. I would recommend reading the book, *The Life Giving Church*, by Ted Haggard who shares how they operate their ministry. I personally feel it is one of the best books on establishing a biblical church government.

The great men of God who have fallen in the last 20 years will tell you that they had no one speaking objectively into their lives. In the Book of Acts the church established an apostolic counsel which they used to question each other to keep the movement pure and right before God. No one man can always make an accurate decision without good counsel around him.

They resist change.

Saul knew that he had lost his kingdom from the time that Samuel had prophesied it to him. But he tried to hang on as long as he could. He would have rather seen the kingdom go down than to see it handed off to someone else. That is the moment when you can tell whether a man is a true leader or a hireling.

When our significance is in the buildings we have built and not in the Christ we serve, then we will do whatever it takes to hold on. We feel we must be the ones to present this ministry we have built with our sweat and blood before God. In reality, God is not interested in the buildings. He is interested in you and the people in the buildings.

What gives you significance? I have asked that question myself. What in my life can I really lay before Jesus someday? It will not be the books I have written; it will not be the ministry I have built; it will not be the earthly possessions I have obtained. It will be the people who I have encouraged and helped while serving out my time on this planet.

When I witness the young men and women who Kim and I have trained for the ministry go and raise up works all over the world, that is what is significant to me. That is what brings me joy—not my accomplishments, but theirs. That is what I pray will stand the test of Jesus' eyes when I stand before him.

Philippians 4:1 says, "Therefore, my beloved and longed-for brethren, my joy and **crown**…" (emphasis added).

Empire builders have few friends.

You are in danger if you become isolated from people. Is a shepherd familiar with his sheep? Do the sheep not know the shepherd by his voice? I have heard much said about the sin of familiarity to the point that some have taken it into a place of their own deception. They will not associate with anyone in the church and choose to keep completely to themselves.

They feel this is the calling to truly lead people. I understand that there is a balance, but we must look closely at the greatest leader who ever walked the earth.

Jesus knew the men he worked with by building a solid relationship with them. He fathered them and released them when it was time. He watched over them and told them He would be with them always, even unto the end of the earth. He was there to affirm them, correct them and love them. They were His friends. *That is why He died for them, and in time they chose to die for Him.*

Empire builders do not know how to release.

When Saul eyed David and his success, he was not willing to let any glory come to David. He wanted it all pointed toward himself. He demanded affirmation from the people but gave none to anyone else, and constantly listened to hear what the people were saying about him. He was not capable of allowing others to be successful nor be a part of his kingdom.

Here are some questions we as leaders have to ask ourselves when we are in the middle of releasing a staff member. This refers to a release and not having to let someone go.

• Are you treating them the way you would desire to be treated if you were leaving?

• Have you carefully studied what Jesus would do in the situation?

• Have you considered the positive things these people have done for you and your ministry?

• Have you adequately compensated them financially to allow them to operate a few months while beginning their new ministry or job?

• Do you have their best interests in mind, or do you have yours in mind?

• Have you left the door open for them to return to your ministry if possible?

• Have you left the door open to them so that you can maintain a relationship with them?

• Have you considered the impact a negative exit will have on them, their family, and their future?

• Have you sought good counsel from other leaders regarding how they release those who have been faithful?

Sometimes we as leaders can get so emotionally involved in a situation that we are not able to make an accurate assessment of the whole situation. We see it only through our eyes. Talk to someone else who can help you see through a different perspective so you can make good decisions.

One of the most difficult things a leader has to face is when God releases good people from us. We have to work hard at not taking it personally. At that time we must let God help us be kingdom minded and not empire minded.

Remember God is merciful, and you never know how God is going to use that person in the future. When you release with blessing, that blessing will come looking for you.

Empire builders are ruled by their own insecurity.

Saul was one of the most insecure leaders ever. He trusted no one. His fear ruled him and dominated his thinking. How many leaders talk about faith and yet are ruled by fear and their own insecurity?

Saul attempted to cut off David and anyone associated with him. This consumed and controlled his thinking every day. Saul was out to erase

David's memory from the people. He claimed that he was doing this for the sake of Jonathan; but the truth was, he was doing it for himself.

As a pastor, how do you respond when God begins to use someone on your staff? How do you respond when a minister on your staff feels God is calling him into another ministry? What actions have you taken to assure that God's perfect will is being done for that person? Are you more concerned about the impact on your ministry or helping these people fulfill their call? I know these are hard questions, but we as leaders have to examine our lives. Can you release them with dignity for the Kingdom of God, or do you go into a protection mode for the empire?

Many a young minister attempting to do the will of God has left hurt, bruised and confused wondering how it happened to him. Some leave the church saying they will never trust leaders again and are no longer continuing to serve in the ministry. A minister from a large independent church confided to me that the things said to him by his pastor during his transition were so hurtful that he could never repeat them.

If you can identify with this, I want to encourage you that God is very just. Don't let offense or hurt rule you. Psalm 17:1-2 says, "Hear a just cause, O Lord....Let my vindication come for Your presence...." Walk away in love and hold your head up high. Watch what God will do in your life. It may be hard right now, but remember if man forsakes you, the Lord will lift you up. The key is to guard your heart and not let the hurt get in. Determine to go and be the spiritual father to others that you've always desired to have.

Empire builders will deal continually with a distressing spirit.

Saul was *one person* one day and *someone else* the next due to the distress he was under. He became controlled by something that began to affect his mind. He was no longer able to function in a real world. He had an irrational mind.

He lived in fear because everything he did to destroy David was not working. First Samuel 18:15 says that David behaved very wisely and Saul was afraid of him. Saul feared that someone was going to take his kingdom away.

An empire builder lives in fear that someone will rise up near them to take their kingdom. They eye the people close by and look constantly for their weaknesses. These are pastors who know little about team ministry and recognizing the true gifts around them. According to their thinking, the pulpit was built for their platform, and no one is going to step into it but them. A staff member should live only for them and what they desire. When a staff member leaves it will always be a break.

The spirit of the leader sets the atmosphere for the productivity of that ministry. If the leader is an empire builder, you will witness people coming only for a while and then they will leave. There will be a big back door. This happens because the people feel no ownership and quickly discover there is no place for them to use their God-given gifts.

These traits ended the kingdom of Saul. It was built on sand. Any ministry that is built around a personality will not stand the test of time. It will have its moment in the sun but will soon fall. Why? It is built for self and not for Jesus.

NOW LET'S TAKE A LOOK AT KINGDOM-MINDED LEADERS

They know how to take the lid off.

If you put fleas in a jar with a lid on it, you will discover that they will jump to get out. But as they hit the lid, they will eventually become *conditioned* to jump only so high. Even when you do take the lid off, they will not jump out.

Kingdom minded leaders desire to minister and motivate people to reach their full potential for God. They want to disciple these people in Christ and see these men and women shine like the sun.

They get excited when disciples come back with reports of all God is doing. They see people as an investment. They are not looking for people who will invest in them before they are invested in.

They refuse to stay in one rut or vein and are constantly searching for ways of increasing their ministry capacity by living outside the box.

I have discovered that God's Kingdom is so big that it can never be fully comprehended. There are men and women doing things that I have never thought of doing. But you have to get outside of your so-called ministry circle or camp to discover it.

When is the last time you went to a church conference where you did not know a soul? Do you attend only those meetings that cater to what you are comfortable with? Are the meetings you attend the ones where you are seated in a reserve section? Have you studied from books that have different viewpoints than yours? Are you afraid of the change that will be required of you to go to the next level?

Kingdom leaders live with the lid off. *Why?* Because God lives with the lid off.

They are men and women of God.

They know that without Jesus they are nothing. As a minister of the gospel I know the exact time when God spoke to my heart to go into the ministry. That calling came from Heaven and not of myself. I know that I am responsible for that calling and will stand before God for that calling.

I must also understand the responsibility of the office I stand in. If I abuse, control, manipulate or dominate people by using that office, God will deal with me.

In Numbers 20 Moses was commanded by God to speak to the rock; however Moses got angry and struck the rock twice. Then the Lord spoke to him in verse 12, "Because you did not believe Me, to hallow Me in the eyes of the children of Israel, therefore you shall not bring this assembly into the land which I have given them."

When you as a leader misrepresent God before the people and misuse the office God has set you into, God will allow you to see your future but you will not be able to go into it.

That is why James 3:1 says, "My brethren, let not many of you become teachers, knowing that we shall receive a stricter judgment." It is an awesome thing to think that God chose you for the ministry. Now how you use that office is up to you, but irregardless, you will stand before the Great Shepherd and be judged. That thought makes me search my heart daily to make sure I have treated people fairly and justly.

Many ministers have had the privilege of seeing what God wanted them to do, but due to their abuse of the office, they stand today looking only at a future that someone else will go into.

They are God pleasers.

Hebrews 11:5 says that Enoch had a testimony of that which pleased God. Enoch according to Genesis 5 walked with God for 300 years and pleased Him. That is an incredible testimony. The Bible says he had sons and daughters, which means he walked with God and pleased Him while raising a family. It is possible to walk with God these days and raise up a godly family.

As a father of three children I know what brings me pleasure and pleases me. Let's look at some of these things so that we can discover more of what pleases God.

• When my children do the little things that need to be done around the house without being told.

• When they come in on time because of respect and honor, and not out of obligation.

• When they treat the home I have provided for them with respect.

• When they show me love and appreciation for what I have done to provide for them.

• When they are bold in the face of adversity.

• When they enjoy my company.

• When they come to me for advice.

• When they receive my instruction and correction.

• When they desire my opinion about their decisions.

• When I see them compassionate toward others who are less fortunate.

• When they ask for my help.

• When they let me know that I am the greatest dad there is.

• When I see the smiles on their faces as I bless them and they are not expecting it.

• When they are at peace with themselves and the life they have.

• When they desire to know the will of God for their lives and fulfill it.

• When they walk in purity and holiness.

• When they sit in my lap and tell me, "I love you, Dad."

All these give me great pleasure as a father. It is the same when we do these for our heavenly Father. My greatest prayer as a leader is that I have a testimony of pleasing God.

They are releasers.

Kingdom-minded leaders have an apostolic mind-set. They know in order for the Kingdom to be established they must train and release. They must follow the example that Jesus set down in training, equipping, mentoring and fathering to see God's Kingdom established in the earth.

They are senders. John 17:18 is a driving force in their lives. "As You [the Father] sent Me into the world, I also have sent them into the world." That spirit rules their lives and their ministry. It is all about building and expanding the Kingdom of God. They look for young men and women in whom they can impart and release for God to use mightily.

This is the very spirit and nature of Christ Himself. He knew the investment in the disciples would eventually pay off. He saw their shortcomings but chose to build on their strengths. He released them to represent Him to the world.

This is what God is saying now to every leader. Are you going to build your kingdom, or are you going to build God's Kingdom? Are you going to release the men and women He is sending you to be all that God wants them to be? Are you going to invest in them and be there for them when they need your help?

The Great Commission says to go and make disciples. That commission has not changed. It is a commission that stands for all of us. We must train them, equip them, bless them and send them.

They are spiritual fathers and mothers.

In Malachi 4:5-6 the Bible says, "Behold, I will send you Elijah the prophet before the coming of the great and dreadful day of the Lord. And he will turn the hearts of the fathers to the children, and the hearts of the children to their fathers."

The apostle Paul said in First Corinthians 4:15, "For though you might have ten thousand instructors in Christ, yet you do not have many fathers." The cry in the land right now is, "Where are all the fathers?"

A father is more than a mentor. The one being simply mentored bears all the responsibility to look to the teacher. I have been mentored in golf, chess, tennis and many other things but not fathered in any of those. It takes more than just being a mentor to be a spiritual father.

The prophet Malachi says that the fathers will turn to the children and the children to the fathers. It is the responsibility of the fathers to turn first to the children before the children will turn back to the fathers. I have heard preached from several pulpits that it is the responsibility of the sons to take care of the fathers. However, as a father I have the first obligation to my children. I am responsible to see to their well-being, education and release into the world. It is no different in the spiritual world.

A young minister and his wife were invited to a home of a prominent minister. This home was as big as most gymnasiums. I am not against having a big home because everything is relevant, and you never know the circumstances behind the blessing of God in a man's life.

While this young minister was there, he was shown around the ministry in order to encourage him to go to another level. That all sounded good until he was finally presented with the reason he was invited there. He was asked to consider being one of the man's spiritual sons. He was told he would need to break off relationships with any other man of God in his life and could look to only this minister for counsel and guidance. But then the real hook came when he was told about the need to sow financially. He was informed that in order for him "to go up," he had to "sow up." That meant he had to first plant a financial seed into the man of God above him in order to get to the level where he was positioned. In other words, he would need to send his personal tithe to the man every month.

I will be the first to say I believe in honoring the men and women of God who have influenced your life by sowing financial seeds to them. First

Timothy 5:17 says, "Let the elders who rule well be counted worthy of double honor, especially those who labor in the word and doctrine." My wife and I have done this many times and have seen God's blessing come back in great measure. But when we go so far as to make this a required arrangement, so that the only way you have access to this ministry is by sowing seeds to them, that is where we have to draw the line. This is nothing more than a spiritual Mafia. We need true spiritual fathers, not godfathers. It's spiritual prostitution when you sow money for favor. I have had men tell me that if they sow $1,000 a month to a certain man of God, they will be given access to his cell phone number. If you are that desperate for someone to speak into your life, I will gladly let you have mine for $500 a month. (I am kidding, of course.) Now you see how far off this is getting.

This pastor had over 200 sons of the ministry sowing their tithe to him personally. As long as they sowed the seed, they could have access to him to receive his counsel. This young minister was asked to sign some papers making it all legal if he decided this is what he wanted to do.

What is sad about this true story is that here we see a revelation of spiritual fathering being corrupted by this kind of teaching. My dad would be insulted if his sons had to support him when he retired. I still, to this day, have to fight with my parents just to pay the dinner bill when we eat out. They want to see me blessed and have sown greatly in finances to see me succeed. When I was released to start *Focus on the Harvest*, they were the first to partner with me. Now that is what a father is all about; it is not the other way around.

Satan will always provide a counterfeit when the Spirit of God is speaking to leaders about a need. We must be men of integrity and sow into our spiritual sons to see them reach their generation for God.

A true spiritual father will rejoice when you succeed and will do whatever it takes to help make you a success for God. He will be there for you in the difficult times and will sincerely help you in any way he can, expecting nothing in return. His reward is your success. That is a true father. In return for the father's love, the son will naturally take care of that father in his older years, due to the love, honor and respect that a son has for his father.

My earthly dad cheered me on when I was sent in to pitch during a game in which my team was losing. I struck out nine batters in a row and won the game. He was so proud of me. The next game I started by hitting the first three batters and walking the next six. My dad was still the one who loved me and encouraged me to continue. It was his love that put me back on the pitching mound.

That type of character is what God is looking for in spiritual fathers. I want you to remember something and never forget it: *Your future will rest, not in your relationship with your peers, but in your relationship with your sons.*

They are people of character.

Jesus preached in Matthew 4:23-24, and multitudes followed Him to see the miracles and signs and wonders. But in Chapter 5 He pulled the disciples aside and began to talk about the attitudes of the heart. I have personally thought that this would have been a great time to talk about how to have a miracle ministry; but Jesus pulled the disciples back to reality. It is not the miracles that make the man; it is the attitudes of the heart.

Character is walking with a humble heart. It is developed by staying close to God and having a checkup with God to determine how you are walking with Him and treating your fellowman. It is praying for God to deal with you. The greatest problem is not the devil; it is you.

Character is built through a repentant heart. When Zaccheus came down to Jesus, he first said, "Lord, please come to my house and forgive me of any sin; and if I have wronged anyone, I will pay them back fourfold" (see Lk. 19:2-8). That is true repentance. If we as leaders have wronged people in the congregation or on our staff, we need to privately apologize and make it right for God's blessing to fully come on us. That is the true test of character.

Character is a true spirit of meekness. I believe kindness is a fruit of meekness—being kind and not demanding of people, giving people permission to make mistakes and helping them when they do. Jesus said, "Learn of Me for I am meek and lowly in heart" (Mt. 11:29 KJV). Meekness is something we must learn. Sometimes we excuse our own personality and expect others to accept it because of our position. We as leaders must strive to be like Christ (meek and lowly in heart). Some of us just have to strive harder than others.

Character is hungering and thirsting after God. It comes from an unquenchable thirst for God and His Word.

Character is the demonstration of mercy. God's goodness and mercy follow us all the days of our lives. God's goodness comes as we walk uprightly before God, and His mercy comes when we have sinned against God. Let the people we lead see the goodness and the mercy of God through our leadership.

Character is walking in purity. It is a pure heart and pure eyes that see God. This is not a future revelation but a present revelation. Those who walk holy in heart, attitude, and body will see God involved in their lives.

Character is being a peacemaker. It is going out of your way to walk in peace with people. It is looking out for their best interest over yours. It is negotiating with people to find a compromise. It is the ability to bring peace to troubled people. *When you set your path to establish peace with people, you will live in peace with yourself.*

Character is acting right and doing right in the middle of being wronged. It is trusting that God is in control of your life, and it a decision not to retaliate.

Character is built when it hurts the most.

They are people of prayer.

Nothing they do is done without seeking the guidance of the Holy Spirit. Their ministry is birthed from their prayer closet. They stay before God in order to represent God to their congregation and staff. They lead through prayer, teach through prayer and pastor through prayer.

Their prayer life reveals their true dependency on God. Revelation 1:10 is one of the most powerful Scriptures for every minister: "I was in the Spirit on the Lord's Day...." It literally means I was at the place to receive divine revelation from God. When is the last time you have been lost in the spirit of prayer? When is the last time you felt the very presence of God in your prayer closet? When is the last time you sensed the presence of the Lord in your pulpit and knew God was all over you?

To have a fresh anointing we must have a freshness in our prayer life.

Let me give a list of other characteristics of a Kingdom leader. You can look at these and examine your own heart.

- *They are men and women of revelation.*

- *They are tried and tested.*

- *They know how to delegate.*

- *They are of a broken and contrite spirit.*

- *They are true shepherds.*

- *They are very relational.*

- *They are called and selected by God.*

- *They are highly motivated.*

- *They are full of compassion.*

- *They walk in love.*

- *They are consistent.*

- *They are builders of people.*

- *They are full of courage.*

- *They are givers.*

- *They are secure in who they are.*

- *They know the people around them.*

- *They are submissive.*

- *Their number-one goal is to be like Christ.*

We can lead people only to the place that we have already been in God. We are not able to take our congregations to a place in Christ that we are not striving for ourselves.

When God called Elijah, it was at Israel's worst time in history. In First Kings 17 Elijah showed up and prophesied by the Spirit of God a word that was going to make an impact in that nation. It is interesting that there is no genealogy mentioned about the man. He appeared at the worst time in the history of Israel and God used him to begin a new thing in that nation. This last-day Church will not be a church based on personalities, but will be Kingdom leaders looking to establish the Kingdom and not a new ministry. The Church has been like the NBA, looking for the next Michael Jordon. God is not looking for just the next new man or woman of God; He is looking for the Church as a whole to rise up and be Kingdom people. This is the day of the saints. Let the Church arise and move the gates of hell.

Elijah came in on a tempest and went out on a whirlwind.

This is a new day for the Body of Christ and the local church.

Chapter 7

IT'S TIME TO...
RELEASE THE MEMBERS INTO THEIR MINISTRY

The Church is not man's idea, but God's. He has set it in order for a clear purpose, and has assigned the Holy Spirit to oversee its activity on earth. That purpose was clearly defined in the first two words of Matthew 28:19 (KJV), "*Go ye.*" This is the season for the Body of Christ to fulfill its God-ordained destiny.

For too many years spiritual leaders have tended sheep rather than train soldiers. Ephesians 4:11-12 says, "And He Himself gave some to be apostles, some prophets, some evangelists, and some pastors and teachers, *for the equipping of the saints for the work of ministry*, for the edifying of the body of Christ. A healthy church is a church busy training and equipping saints to take the message of Christ outside the walls of the sanctuary into the marketplace where the un-churched live.

Ted Haggard, pastor of New Life Church in Colorado Springs, spoke a powerful truth when he said, "It is time for pastors to pastor the staff, the staff to pastor the congregation, and the congregation to pastor the city." I believe this is a good description of a healthy church.

God wants His Church built on purpose, not personality.

In the last few decades, many congregations have built God's church on personality, rather than spiritual purpose. This has caused many immature believers to constantly run to and fro, attempting to identify who the next spiritual giant will be. Rather than linking up with a local body, becoming trained with God-given purpose, and being released into marketplace ministry, they waste time looking for a new revelation and seeking a new, exciting leader to take them into the next move of God.

Friend, the day of the celebrity preacher is over. Those in the church who bought into the idea that these chosen men and women are the only ones who possess gifts of God, set themselves up for disappointment. Servants of God should not be put on a pedestal and treated like a rock star. A pedestal is a lonely place to be, and it's easy to fall from such an exalted position. I've known believers who thought if they could just get to one of these celebrated ministers they could get the answer they needed from God. It grieves the Holy Ghost that we have taken our eyes off the Lord and put them on these mortal men and women.

Yes, God absolutely sets His government in the church. He calls and appoints leaders to guide and care for it. He sets in place a fivefold ministry gifting for building up His Body, and equipping it for the work of ministry. But we all must keep in mind that it is God's Church, God's ministry, and God's glory, manifested in the earth. Honor God's leaders, but don't make the mistake of heaping onto created man the praise deserved only by the Creator.

God wants to take back areas currently under satan's control.

Look around your home church on Sunday morning. Only two percent of the people you see work in full-time ministry as a vocation. These people are paid a salary to conduct the business of the church body. That leaves 98 percent whose salary comes from activities in business, education, or government. What has occurred over the years is this: satan has been willing to give us a couple hours on Sunday morning to try and convince the 98 percent they need Jesus. It's the remainder of the week he is not willing to give up without a fight. He loves his power over the workplace, his control over business, education, and government. Unfortunately, many buy into his lie that the church is God's and the marketplace is satan's. We hire a good pastor, one we like to hear speak, go sit on a church pew a couple hours a week, then go our merry way, satisfied with having done our religious duty.

In doing this, we totally miss the plan God put into action for the Church on the day of Pentecost. He has set leaders in the Body to train and equip saints to go into their workplace to take back what the enemy has stolen from mankind. His plan is that the two percent train up an army to establish Kingdom principles in every area of life. No more will the majority of ministry be from the pulpit; God is releasing it in the pew.

I was raised in a Pentecostal church. How excited we used to get singing the old gospel songs. "I'll Fly Away" or "When We All Get to Heaven" brought chill bumps as we stood with our hands extended, shouting victory because someday Jesus was coming to get us out of this mess we call the world.

But we missed the point. He will come for us at His appointed time, but until that day we are to stay busy taking territory from the enemy. We have been told to occupy until He comes, establishing the Kingdom of God on planet earth.

I am not of the persuasion that the world we inhabit will only get darker. I do not believe we should just sit quietly and let it happen, that there is nothing we can do about it. Yes, the Bible is clear that sin will abound in the latter days. In fact, sin has been thriving since the Garden of Eden, but Romans 5:20 (NIV) assures us "where sin increased, grace increased all the more." As we exit the pews in victory each Lord's Day, marching as an army into the enemy's territory, His grace will flourish, producing life in the marketplace.

Whether housewife or student, educator or government employee, white or blue-collar worker, get excited about the work of God and develop your ministry gifting. I believe the next move of God's Spirit will be the Body of Christ using those gifts, going into their workplace, and possessing it for the Kingdom of God.

God is practical. He knew from the beginning there would be only certain places a full-time minister could go. Can you imagine the confusion if preachers would don hard hats and try to minister on a construction site? What would happen if I jumped up in the middle of a company business meeting and began to deliver the gospel? Or interrupted a doctor in the operating room? There are places I will never be able to go, just as there are places you will never go. But the wisdom of God can cross any barrier, can go onto any job site, can show up in any school cafeteria. How? Through that 98 percent of the congregation who has been trained and equipped to take the gospel to their world. You will meet people I will never meet, talk to people I will never talk to, go places I will never go. That is your ministry, your workplace.

We are moving into a season of release.

The Body of Christ is moving into a new season of God's anointing. Recently, I was in prayer seeking the Lord for a word concerning the upcoming year. While worshipping and fellowshipping with the Lord, the Holy Spirit began to speak: "*I'm not giving you a word just for this year because I do not move in years. I move in seasons.*" I thought about Galatians 6:9 (KJV), "In due season we shall reap, if we faint not," and Ecclesiastes 3:1, "To everything there is a season."

That truth spoke to me, and I knew the Holy Spirit had shown me something. But I wanted to know more. How long is a season? How will I recognize when it comes or when it's over? I began to see that God's time frame for a season is simply *from the beginning to the end*.

The Lord began to talk to me about the Body of Christ. He said that we are moving into *a season of release*. He reminded me of the caterpillar metamorphosing into the butterfly. He said to me, "*This is not just a release out of, but a release into.*" The caterpillar knows instinctively when change is ready to occur. That worm forms a cocoon to begin its process of metamorphosis. He knows without question he was not destined to crawl forever; he was designed to fly.

Maybe you can identify with that caterpillar. You feel wrapped in a cocoon of difficulty and see no way out. But know this: A cocoon can be a prison or a sanctuary. Your attitude will determine your season of confinement. Murmuring and complaining magnifies your problems, turning the cocoon into a prison. But praise and thanksgiving to God turns your cocoon into a sanctuary and will bring you into a season of release.

God is liberating us from our past to free us for our future. He has somewhere better for us to go. Yet we are always trying to go there on our own. The Body of Christ spends millions every year on recreation, on medicine, on travel, on a thousand other things to get relief from the pressure we live under. We run constantly to seminars to learn: How to Get Your Healing, How to Get Out of Debt, How to Fight Depression, How to Eat Right. We are always looking to find our miracle cure. But how many of us spend much time at all equipping ourselves to fulfill the assignment God has given us as believers?

Amazing, isn't it, to study the great men and women of faith listed in the chapter 11 of Hebrews? While they went about fulfilling their God-called destinies, He supplied all their needs. These faith heroes did not waste time whining to God about their problems. As they stayed busy doing Kingdom work, the King kept busy blessing them. You see, *when you get involved in God's harvest, God gets involved in yours.*

We all want God's best. Many have been sitting, waiting years to receive it. But they are missing a principle that is the basis of the story of Jesus and the ten lepers, found in Luke 17. They heard He was coming; and standing at a great distance, the lepers cried loudly for His help. Jesus told them to go show themselves to the priest. And here is the key: *"As they went, they were cleansed."* Action on the part of the lepers brought about their healing. This is a truth the Holy Spirit is speaking today. As you begin

to go and fulfill the assignment God has placed upon your life; your healing, deliverance, and prosperity will come.

HARVEST PRINCIPLES TO MOVE INTO MINISTRY

"The harvest truly is plentiful, but the laborers are few. Therefore pray
the Lord of the harvest to send out laborers into His harvest." Jesus' words,
spoken to His disciples in Matthew 9:37-38, were heartfelt. As He traveled
through villages, He saw multitudes of tired, weary human beings.
Compassion moved Him to speak of them in harvest terms. I see in these
verses, and the first few verses of chapter 10, some keys to help us move
into marketplace ministry.

Key Number One: We must have eyes to see the harvest.

Until we see people as harvest—the way Jesus saw them—we cannot
pray the way Jesus said to pray.. He told us to pray to the Lord of the harvest, that He would send laborers into His harvest. When we look at our
city, our country, or even another nation, how do we see the lost? Do we
say, "Look at them, they belong to the devil, and act just like him"? Or do
we say, "Jesus, You are the Lord of this harvest. You called it *Your* harvest,
and I'm getting in agreement with You. Now, I pray You will send laborers
into *Your* harvest field"?

When Jesus used harvest terminology, He was speaking of souls, not
money. Not long ago, I telephoned a ministry, and when the secretary
answered, I identified myself as Terry Nance of Focus on the Harvest
Ministry. I thought the secretary was going to shout when she heard the
name of my ministry. She loved it, she told me, because she had been focusing on "her harvest," calling it in from the north, south, east, and west.

Do you understand what she said? She was calling in her harvest,
which in her heart was money. It's not her fault, really. Many ministers have
talked about harvest as being money for so long that, when it is preached,

people see only green. But when Jesus talked about harvest in the New Testament, He always meant souls.

There was strong passion behind Jesus' words when He instructed us to pray that workers would be "sent out." The English word *send* is weaker than the original Greek word. Strong's Concordance definition is "to thrust, to cast out, to evict, and to eject." Many of us in Pentecostal and Charismatic churches can get excited about Strong's definition if we are talking about devils. We say, "Let's thrust them out, cast them out; let's evict them, even eject them." But Jesus was not talking about devils; He was telling the Church to pray that God would thrust laborers into His harvest field to gather in souls.

My prayer for these last days is that God will move in the local church, that He will thrust you into the harvest, that He will cast you into the harvest, that He will evict you into the harvest, and eject you into the harvest. Church, are you willing to begin praying that prayer in faith?

What does it mean to be evicted? Basically, it means to be thrown into the streets. Can you see that is the heart of God today for the Church? Jesus wants us to pray the Holy Spirit will evict us from our comfortable church pew, thrust us into the streets, and cast us into the marketplace, where He will use us mightily to bring in His harvest, to manifest His glory for all to see.

A few years ago, I was vacationing in Branson, Missouri with my family. As we were driving down the street, the kids noticed a ride that looked exciting, at least to them. It was called the Ejection Seat. Let me explain this "fun" ride to you. As two people sit in the seat, they are strapped in and then catapulted into the air a good hundred feet, where they are then released to freefall toward the earth. When they reach bottom, the straps, like giant rubber bands, shoot them back toward the heavens.

Well, when my son Alex, who I introduced you to in Chapter 4, saw the ride, he began to plead with me, "Please, Dad. Please, Dad. Please, please, please ride with me. Ride with me."

"Don't even go there," I told him. "There is no way on this planet I'm riding that thing with you."

Ha! Then my wife and daughter got involved. Before I knew it, everyone in the car was after me. I almost felt my manhood being challenged.

The question I asked, "Why me?" never got answered. The vote was four to one…Dad should ride.

After some real negotiating, it was obvious I was being set up. I finally agreed to drive over and look at the ride. I thought it had looked big from our position on the road, but that was nothing to this up-close and personal observation. Looking at this thing, I was sure it could sling you into the third heaven, the one where Paul saw Jesus.

There was a row of people waiting to ride, and I found myself in the same line with Alex. As we waited, the ride ended for a couple who got off looking peaked, and the man immediately bent over and threw up. As I glanced around, I noticed that those folks who had been waiting to ride suddenly disappeared. It was just Alex and me. Looking at my family, the workers, and even the strangers, I generously offered to pay for anyone's ride, if they would take my place. No one volunteered. And my family continued to nag.

"Okay, I'll do it," I said in my most aggravated tone, "if you will just be quiet." As they strapped me into that ejection seat, I began to ask Jesus to forgive me for any sin I may have committed.

But not Alex. He was jumping all over the place with excitement because he was going for the ride of his life. Suddenly it lifted you up. You could hear the bands tightening. I had a revelation of commitment; there was no turning back. Then BANG! We were gone. Spinning like a top we flew through the air stretching the bands until they would stretch no more; then we began the free fall, leaving our stomachs somewhere in the air. We reached the bottom; then, without even time to sigh with relief, we shot toward the clouds again. After the third trip up, I was beginning to relax, when I heard Alex, with his Romanian accent say, "I don't like this. I didn't know it would be like this. I want to get down." It didn't take me a second to remind him whose idea it was in the first place and to let him know it was a little late to change his mind.

Folks, this is a good picture of where many of us are in the Body of Christ. We cry out in prayer, "Oh, God, please thrust me into the harvest. Oh, God, please cast me into the harvest. Oh, God, please evict and eject me into the harvest." And when God does so, it's not long before we quickly determine, "I don't like this. I didn't know it would be like this."

Many times we see the excitement of gathering in the harvest, but have no revelation of the commitment it takes to work the fields. When God thrusts us forth, we must be ready for warfare, because satan will do his best to send us back to pew-sitting. Warfare in these last days will intensify, not decrease. But the Lord of the harvest, who ejects us into His fields, will never leave us or forsake us. His heart is in His harvest.

Jesus' concern is pictured vividly in *The Message* translation of Matthew 9:36-37 and 10:1:

> *What a huge harvest! He said to His disciples. How few the workers! On your knees and pray for harvest hands! The prayer was no sooner prayed than it was answered. Jesus called His twelve followers and sent them into the ripe fields.*

I love the way *The Message* describes this event. With His heart breaking at the size of the harvest, Jesus cried out to His disciples to get on their knees and pray for harvest hands. *"The prayer was no sooner prayed than it was answered."* Jesus immediately called twelve, the very twelve who prayed the prayer, and commissioned them to become the answer, to go begin gathering in His harvest. The Church needs to pray that prayer while looking in the mirror, because we are the harvest hands He is sending forth.

Why is it important that each church unite behind their pastor? Why is it important we develop our gifts and talents and use them in the local church? Why is it important we get out of our comfort zones? Why is it important we take the challenge and run with the vision of the house?

Why is it important to recognize and submit to spiritual authority? The answer: HARVEST

During harvest season something happens in the hearts of the workers:

1. Everyone works.

2. Long hours are required to gather the crop.

3. Complaining and murmuring are forgotten (too much work to complain).

4. Unity is a must.

5. Determination is the motivator.

6. Pain is forgotten (no time to think on it).

7. Joy, self-esteem, peace, satisfaction, and laughter are the rewards.

Key Number Two: We must go with the authority of Jesus.

Jesus did not just send out the twelve empty-handed. He gave them something powerful to work with. Matthew 10:1 says, "…He gave them power over unclean spirits, to cast them out, and to heal all kinds of sickness and all kinds of disease."

Other than His death and resurrection, which purchased salvation for mankind, the most vital task Jesus accomplished while on earth was to invest Himself in twelve men who would continue the work when He went back to His Father. He trained them, equipped them, and then gave them His own authority to establish the Church.

We look at Jesus' life and remember the miracles and healings He released into those broken people He described as harvest. Those events were directly tied to the authority He walked in while on earth. What if He would have only lived, died, performed miracles, and then went back to Heaven? The work would have ended 2,000 years ago.

But Jesus trained men, and gave them His power and authority to build the Church and cover the world with His glory. I have been in and around charismatic churches for over 25 years. One of the central messages of this movement has been that people should take back the dominion God gave to Adam and Eve in Genesis 1:28:

> *Then God blessed them, and God said to them, "Be fruitful and multiply; fill the earth and subdue it; have dominion over the fish of the sea, over the birds of the air, and over every living thing that moves on the earth."*

So we tell our congregations, "Go take dominion over the devil. Heal the sick. Get financially prosperous. Be healthy, wealthy, and wise." And there is nothing wrong with any of those things. But when God told Adam and Eve to take dominion, He gave them a specific plan: "*Be fruitful and multiply.*"

The key to Adam and Eve taking authority and dominion over the earth was in reproduction. It was through giving birth to sons and daughters, and then releasing them to procreate, that their dominion was to be guaranteed for generations. *There is no dominion without reproduction.*

God's plan has not changed. The key to establishing the Kingdom of God on earth is through the same process. We as leaders must use the example of Jesus with the twelve. We must raise up sons and daughters, train and equip them, then release them to go. In this way, the time and training you have invested will be multiplied in the earth.

True success in God's Kingdom is not measured by the size of your congregation, but by the sons and daughters you have trained, equipped, and released into harvest. Imitate Jesus. Be willing to thrust out workers with the "go ye" attitude He perfected on earth.

Are you a generational, or seasonal, thinker in ministry? Do you understand your work can last for a season, or will you build for generations to come? Seasonal ministry is short-lived because it is bound by control. But that fivefold ministry gift willing to train, equip, and release, will build for generations to come. We as ministers of God must reproduce our-selves, give away the authority God gave us, and provide a platform for our sons and daughters to succeed. As a minister of God, what have you done to help your spiritual sons and daughters find success?

I am the father of three children. Recently, my oldest daughter, McCall, shared with me her desire to attend college and her plans for her future. I told her, "I am your dad, and I will do everything in my power to help you get your education, in order to succeed in life. I am here for you and will do all I can to help you."

A spiritual father is no different than a natural father. We should do all we can to provide for the success of our sons and daughters. It is unnatu-ral to expect a child to be responsible to the father, unless the father has first been responsible to the child. Jesus not only released His disciples with His authority, but He promised to be with them always, even until the end of the earth.

Just as the fivefold ministry must be willing to release authority, the Body of Christ must be willing to receive it. The power Jesus left with the Church is the ability to overcome the works of the devil. I feel many times we pray for God to get us out of something Jesus has already paid the price for us to overcome. We need to spend the time it takes to understand exactly what Jesus redeemed us from, and begin to thank and praise Him for that redemption.

A pastor friend of mine was invited to speak to a congregation in Europe. The leaders of the church where he would minister sent him a train ticket that was in a language he could not read. On the day of his departure, he worked his way through crowded aisles, past almost empty, first-class cabins to find a seat in a compartment crammed full of people, all of them smoking. Through the entire trip, crossing from one country into another, he kept thinking about those first-class cabins he had passed, with big no-smoking signs in the windows. On the other hand, he knew that the folks who had invited him had a limited budget and so he reminded himself to be content with the ticket they had sent him.

When he arrived at his destination, the people questioned him about his trip. He didn't want to complain, or sound ungrateful, but he casually mentioned the challenge he had with the crowded smoke-filled cabin. His hosts were shocked. They asked to see his receipt and ticket stub. How surprised the minister was to learn he was carrying a first-class ticket the entire time. The language barrier had kept him from understanding just what was in his possession.

This story depicts many believers within the Church. We have first-class tickets to travel through this earth journey, yet we sit in the smoking car of life, allowing satan to choke us to death. How many challenges could be averted if we would just take the time to read the Bible, discover the authority Jesus has left with us when He exited this planet, and begin to establish that authority in our lives with prayer and thanksgiving? All power and authority were given to Jesus by His Father. He in turn has delegated them to His disciples. That's us, folks.

McKenna, my youngest daughter, came running into the house one day, so excited. She had found a stray cat in the neighborhood. "Daddy, can I bring him in the house?" Her little eyes pled with me.

However, I quickly put a stop to her plans. "McKenna, darling, I love you, but you are not about to bring that animal into my house. NOT IN MY HOUSE!"

Now, I am not an animal hater, but I was not going to allow anyone to bring a stray cat into my house—not even my daughter. When she becomes an adult, and has her own house, she can bring in anything she wants. But not now.

It is time we rise up, face the devil, and let him know once and for all, "NOT IN MY HOUSE! I am not going to be ruled by you or any of your demonic forces because Jesus has set me free. I am using the authority He gave me." We must stop complaining about our lives, our jobs, our families, the circumstances we encounter every day.

Not long ago, a lady said to me, "Brother Terry, pray for me that God will give me another job. I have to work in the world with a bunch of heathens. I have to listen to their awful talk and hear them take God's name in vain. I want to work in a Christian environment, surrounded by good people."

Doing my best not to hurt her feelings, I explained that God is not interested in her working around only Christian people. God has called her to be the light and salt of the world. She was to take authority over the atmosphere where she was working, and begin to ask God to use her to win those in her office to Jesus. We prayed together and she returned with new excitement into the harvest field where God had placed her.

Many of us are just like that lady, complaining to God and begging Him for deliverance. But escape is not what we need. Gratefulness is! We need to begin to thank God we have a job. Instead of complaining about our boss, asking God to make him resign, let's pray to be used to bless him. Do work with excellence. Be punctual. And by exhibiting these good work habits and characteristics, the hearts of our coworkers will be open to the gospel. We must use the authority we have in Christ to bind demonic influence in our workplace remembering that all things work together for our good because we are the called according to His purpose.

And then we see the kind of people chosen to be His disciples in Matthew 10:2-3: fishermen, tax collectors, and farmers. Regular people. It's quite interesting that the men Jesus selected to be the foundation of the Church were ordinary people from the workplace. Why? Because the religious society in those days had completely lost touch with where the people lived. Again today, God is reaching into the pews and selecting common, everyday people to take the gospel to their world.

Key Number Three: Jesus Call Us and He Sends Us

"These twelve Jesus sent out..." (Mt. 10:5). "Sent" in the Greek, is *apostello*, from which we get the word *apostle*. It simply means being a sent one or one sent on a mission.

"Yes, Brother Terry," you might say, "those disciples were called by Jesus. They were His apostles. But I'm not so sure that I am called."

Yes, you are! We all are called. In John 17:18, Jesus prayed to His Father. "As You sent [*apostello*] Me into the world, I also have sent them into the world." Then in verse 20 He continued, "I do not pray for these alone, but also for those who will believe in Me through their word." God is an apostolic God. He sent Jesus; Jesus sent the Holy Ghost; and the Holy Ghost is sending the Church.

You are a sent one by the Holy Spirit to go into your workplace and do an apostolic work in your daily environment. For years we have heard it preached that it was the apostles who turned the world upside down. There is no question that God anointed them with power to give birth to the Church. But they did not act alone. Acts 8:1 gives us a bigger picture: "Now Saul was consenting to his death. At that time a great persecution arose against the church which was at Jerusalem; and they were all scattered throughout the regions of Judea and Samaria, except the apostles."

This Scripture depicts two different aspects of the Church. You see a *gathered* Church and a *scattered* Church. In the beginning of the Church age, a corporate anointing rested upon the Body of believers as they gathered together to worship God. But the gospel was not delivered to other regions by the gathered Church, but rather by the scattered Church. Verses 4-6 say, "Therefore those who were scattered went everywhere preaching the word. Then Phillip went down to the city of Samaria and preached Christ to them. And the multitudes with one accord heeded the things spoken by Philip, hearing and seeing the miracles which he did."

The scattered Church went everywhere, preaching the Word; and God confirmed that Word with signs following. Even though God kept the apostles in Jerusalem, He released the scattered Church to go into their workplaces with His power and might.

You see, God's Kingdom cannot and will not be contained within the walls of the local church. A true kingdom vision is not to fill a church building with people; it is to take the entire community for God.

When Philip went to Samaria, he went as one of the scattered Church, as a believer into the workplace. As we read the account of the scattered Church in Acts, it is evident to us, 2,000 years later, that the gift of an evangelist was upon him; but when Philip went out, he went as a believer. He needed no title, no special favor from man. The word burning in his heart, and a workplace to share it, were enough.

The next move of the Holy Spirit on the earth will be the Church in *a season of release*, doing the work of the ministry in places of business, education, and government. I see God releasing an army prepared for these last days to encounter all that hell can throw at us, coming forth with victory after victory. The Lord is releasing the anointing, which has in the past been evident in the pulpit, into the saints sitting in the pews.

There is quite a difference in what I observe when standing in a pulpit on a given Sunday morning to share God's Word, and what the man and woman of God in the pew observe.

- From a pew to the pulpit you see a man called of God…from the pulpit to the pew I see people called of God.

- From the pew to the pulpit you see a man anointed of God… from the pulpit to the pew I see a people anointed of God.

- From the pew to the pulpit you see a man called to lead… from the pulpit to the pew I see a people called to lead.

- From the pew to the pulpit you see a man with gifts and talents…from the pulpit to the pew I see people with gifts and talents.

• From the pew to the pulpit you see a man behind a pulpit... from the pulpit to the pew I see a people who have a pulpit (your workplace).

• From the pew to the pulpit you see a man who is a minister of God...from the pulpit to the pew I see people who are ministers of God.

• From the pew to the pulpit you see a man who has a destiny...from the pulpit to the pew I see a people with a destiny.

• From the pew to the pulpit you see a man who you expect to have an active prayer life...from the pulpit to the pew I see a people who should have an active prayer life.

Prior to standing in a pulpit to preach to a congregation, I spend several hours in prayer and study, in which I seek God's will for the meeting and ask Him to direct me, and to make happen what He desires for the people. Why do I do this? Because it is my workplace, and I earn a salary to provide for my family in this workplace. It is what I am gifted to do.

How can you actively prepare for Kingdom living in your workplace?

• Pray that God will live through you each day.

• Pray for God to be evident each day, and let peace guide your heart.

• If at all possible, find a moment or two during a break time to whisper a prayer asking God's blessing on the business.

• Dedicate your workplace to God...watch what He will do.

• Be on time at work...be diligent.

• Do not make a show of your Christianity...Jesus was not religious, neither should you be.

• Simply be yourself. Release God's power in your prayer closet. Then be quiet and let God do the rest.

Jesus said we are the salt of the earth. When God looks at the local church, I believe He sees a big bag of salt. He wants to take the bag, shake it up, and then use that bag of salt to season your entire city. You, friend, are the salt of the earth. Stay salty!

God's Word tells us the kingdoms of this world will become the kingdom of our Lord, and of His Christ. And we, as Kingdom children, will reign forever and ever with Christ. But we don't have to wait. He has called us and is sending us in this season to release His Kingdom in the earth.

Key Number Four: Go to the lost sheep.

Jesus' heart is always for the lost. Remember the parable of the lost sheep? He left the 99 to search for just one. His focus was on the one that was nowhere to be found. In verse 6 of Matthew 10, He told His disciples, "But go rather to the lost sheep of the house of Israel." Jesus has no interest in watching His local Church grow through transfer growth. Obviously, there will always be limited growth due to people moving in and out of areas, but we are foolish if we think big numbers due to saints moving from body to body brings joy to the heart of God. He did not say go from sheepfold to sheepfold. He said go to the lost sheep. God wants His Church in the marketplace, winning souls.

I recently attended an intercessory prayer meeting in a city I was visiting. As the pastor led the congregation, I paid attention so I could be in agreement with him. During half of the prayer time, we prayed for attendance, the youth, the children, the choir, the office staff, the pastors, and their families. The other half was spent praying for finances. When we finished, I thought to myself, *Not one time did we ask God to help us reach the lost in this city.*

What has happened to the Church in America? What has caused us to become so self-centered that we no longer have eyes to see a lost and dying world? Even though there are exceptions, as I travel across our nation, I hear very little about plans to take a city for God. I'm afraid the majority of the Body of Christ has stopped praying for the lost because they are consumed with themselves.

I can't remember the last time I turned on Christian television and heard people talk about winning the lost of their city. Instead, the programs are usually telling us how to get out of debt, how to win over depression, or some other subject that is totally self-absorbed. We are so fixated on ourselves that we have lost our ability to care for those dying around us.

When did you last take time as you drove to work to ask God to use you that day to minister to those around you? I challenge you to prepare yourself each day in prayer and Bible reading; then wait and watch God give you the opportunity to share the message of Jesus.

In Luke 16, Jesus tells the story of a beggar named Lazarus who was laid each day at the gate of a rich man. When Lazarus died, he was carried by angels into Abraham's bosom; but this was not the case for the rich man. Jesus said he died and went to hell where he was tormented in fire. Verses 23-24 say, "And being in torment in Hades, he lifted up his eyes and saw Abraham afar off, and Lazarus in his bosom. They he cried and said, 'Father Abraham, have mercy on me, and send Lazarus that he may dip the tip of his finger in water and cool my tongue; for I am tormented in this flame.' " But Abraham declared this was impossible, because of the justice of God. Then the rich man begged Abraham to send Lazarus back to earth and warn his five brothers who were still living, that they would not come to this horrible place. Again, Abraham declared this could not be done.

Here we witness a man in hell interceding for his loved ones. From hell, he was begging Abraham to send laborers to warn them. This is amazing to me. Hell is filled with intercessors, crying day and night for someone to tell their loved ones not to come where they are. But God does not hear the cries of the dead; He hears the prayers of the living.

We who are alive, are called to pray for our church, our city, our nation, and the world.

If My people, who are called by My name, will humble themselves, and pray and seek My face, and turn from their wicked ways, then I will hear from heaven, and will forgive their sin and heal their land (2 Chronicles 7:14).

God will heal our educational system, government, business sector, and our workplaces when we humble ourselves, get the sin out of our lives, and pray for God to pour His Holy Spirit upon our land.

Key Number Five: Freely you have received, freely give.

Jesus shared this last key as He was thrusting His disciples into the harvest field. This truth is critical as we move into this *season of release*.

You cannot give what you do not have. God does not expect it of you. Don't condemn yourself for what you cannot do. Instead, look at what is in your hand to give. Take inventory of your life and see what you personally can do to establish the Kingdom of God on the earth. Everyone has something to give to God. Look closely. Don't despise the small thing God has put in your life to give away. Whether money, work, or time, freely give it to God.

Last Christmas my wife, Kim, and another family member ran into Wal-Mart to pick up a last-minute item. While standing in line to pay, they noticed a couple with three small children in front of them, their basket full of groceries and gifts. But there was a problem. The man's payroll check would not clear. He then gave them his credit card, but the card was over the limit. Obviously he was humiliated, and his wife was crushed. It was Christmas Eve. There would be no Christmas meal, and the children would get no gifts.

As they left, Kim and Tammy chased them down. They told them not to be ashamed, that all of us sometime in our lives have been in unpleasant situations. They took them back into the store and paid for the groceries and gifts. The wife began to cry, saying no one had ever done anything like this for them.

After they had loved on the family, and ministered to them in prayer, the man turned to Kim and said something I will never forget, *"Someday, I will do the same for someone else that you have done for me."*

Church, this is what Jesus is saying to us. *"Freely receive what I've done for you, and then, just as freely give it away."* There are people in your neighborhood, in your city, your country, and the world just like that couple Kim ministered to. People are crying for help spiritually, physically, and emotionally. We have the answer inside us, given to us freely by a loving Father. Freely we have received; what a delight to freely give.

We are living in exciting times. God is moving in unprecedented ways. He says in the Book of Acts that He will pour out His Spirit on all men. Every one of us is a candidate for this great outpouring. But remember this: God is not pouring out this great harvest of blessing so you can live in a bigger house and drive a luxury car. You are blessed to be a blessing, to assist in bringing in this great harvest of souls Jesus so freely died for.

The vision of the house, the Body of Christ, must be a Kingdom vision. It must reach outside the walls of the local church. It must train, equip, and release God's people into their workplace, to establish His Kingdom on earth. Jesus is returning for a glorious Church. It is time to rise up and go forth in the plans and purpose God has for us.

My prayer is that you will get yourself plugged in to your pastor's vision, which is the vision of the house, and then take what is in you and release it into your world.

May God's grace be mightily upon you as you go.

To contact the author for *Armorbearer* materials such as tapes and videos, for additional materials by Terry Nance, or to schedule an Armorbearer Leadership School in your church or area, write or call:

TERRY NANCE
FOCUS ON THE HARVEST, INC.
P.O. BOX 7087
SPRINGDALE, AR 72766

PHONE:
(479) 872-0777

WEBSITE:
www.godsarmorbearer.com

EMAIL ADDRESS:
tnance@focusontheharvest.com

GOD'S ARMORBEARER STUDY GUIDE

Based on the best-selling book, *God's Armorbearer*, Terry Nance now relases a companion Study Guide that will empower readers with the Word, while expounding on vital principles from the books. Filled with thought-provoking questions, *God's Armorbearer Study Guide* will help you find the answers from God's Word that bring the understanding you desire.

ISBN: 0-971919-33-X

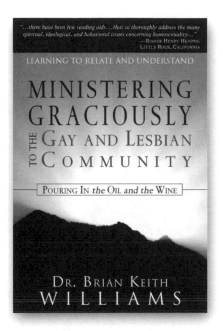